Michael Harris • David Mo

WORLD CLASS

LEVEL 4

STUDENTS' BOOK

Longman

Summary of course content

Learning to learn

A Organise your learning
Students' Book

Learner training	Classroom activity survey
	Organising grammar notes
Speaking/Reading	Book quiz

Activity Book

Listening	Description of classroom activities

B Understanding English
Students' Book

Learner training	Listening strategies/Mini-dictionary/Vocabulary books
Listening/Speaking	Interviewing learners

Activity Book

Listening	Description of listening problems

C Speaking and writing
Students' Book

Learner training	Speaking strategies
Pronunciation	Phonetic symbols/Phonetic bingo
Writing	Note to teacher

Activity Book

Learner training	Writing strategies/Assessing speaking
Pronunciation	Phonetic symbols/Phonetic crossword

Module 1: Fashion

1 What's 'in'
Students' Book

Speaking/Reading	Fashion survey/History of fashion
Language focus	**Comparison: comparative and superlative adjectives/as . . . as**
Writing	Fashion project: description

Activity Book

Listening	Descriptions of clothes
Pronunciation	Word stress/Sounds: /e/ /ɪ/ /ə /i:/
Language practice	**Comparison**

2 Looking good
Students' Book

Speaking/Listening	Shopping/Dialogue: in clothes shop
Function focus	Buying clothes
Learner training	Dictionary use: phrasal verbs
Pronunciation	Sounds: /ə/ /ɪ/
Writing	Fashion project: designing jacket

Activity Book

Language revision	**Personal pronouns/Too and enough**

3 A megamodel
Students' Book

Reading	Magazine article: top model
Language focus	**Just/recently/still/yet/already**
Writing	Fashion project: modelling

Activity Book

Language practice	**Just/recently/still/yet/already**

4 Dressed to kill
Students' Book

Speaking/Listening	Animals and fashion
Language focus	**Present simple/Present continuous (stative and dynamic verbs)**
Pronunciation	Consonant clusters
Writing	Fashion project: listing products

Activity Book

Pronunciation	Plural endings: /s/ /z/
Language practice	**Present simple/Present continuous**

5 Appearances matter
Students' Book

Reading	Poem / Fiction extract
Function focus	Describing people/Describing game
Writing	Description of a person

Activity Book

Language revision	**Adjective order**
Listening	First impressions of people

6 Fluency
Students' Book

Listening	Correcting Cinderella story
Learner training	Speaking strategies: shopping
Speaking	Shopping roleplay
Pronunciation	Linking: /j/ /w/ /r/
Writing	Formal letter/Project display

Activity Book

Listening	Dialogue: shopping

7 Revision
Students' Book

Language practice	(From the module)
Vocabulary	Adjectives/Wordbuilding: prefixes
Learner training	Module check
Language revision	**Test yourself**

Activity Book

Language revision	**Test yourself/Present tenses**

Module 2: Islands

8 Island holidays
Students' Book

Reading	Tourist brochure: Barbados
Listening	Dialogue: travel agent's
Function focus	Asking for holiday information
Writing	Notes about a holiday place

Activity Book

Language revision	**Questions/Question words**
Pronunciation	Intonation with questions

9 Exploring Barbados
Students' Book

Listening	Conversation with tour guide
Language focus	**Review of prepositions**
Pronunciation	Sentence stress
Writing	Directions/Description

Activity Book

Language practice	**Prepositions**
Learner training	Phonetic symbols

10 Life on Skye
Students' Book

Reading	Informal letter
Language focus	**Present perfect simple/continuous**
Speaking	Present and past activities
Writing	Informal letter

Activity Book

Listening	Telephone conversation
Language practice	**Present perfect simple/continuous**

11 Lord of the Flies
Students' Book

Reading	Extracts from *Lord of the Flies*
Listening	Discussions: survival situations
Language focus	**Conditionals review**

Activity Book

Language practice	**Conditionals**
Pronunciation	Sounds: /aɪ/ /iː/ /eɪ/ /e/ /æ/

12 Island survival
Students' Book

Listening	Story: *Lord of the Flies*
Function focus	Agreeing and disagreeing
Pronunciation	Intonation: strong/hesitant

Activity Book

Language revision	**Agreeing:** *so/neither*
Pronunciation	Intonation: certain/uncertain

13 Fluency
Students' Book

Listening	Radio programme/Treasure hunt
Learner training	Accents/Interactive listening
Speaking	Survey/Giving directions
Writing	Description of an island

Activity Book

Listening	Directions
Writing	Postcards/Directions

14 Revision
Students' Book

Language practice	(From the module)
Vocabulary	Wordbuilding: suffixes/Verb *get*
Pronunciation	Sounds: /aɪ/ /iː/ /ɪ/
Learner training	Module check
Language revision	**Test yourself**

Activity Book

Language revision	**Test yourself/Auxiliaries**

Module 3: Crime

15 Crazy crimes
Students' Book

Reading	Newspaper reports
Vocabulary	Phrasal verbs
Function focus	Prohibition
Speaking	Rating crimes

Activity Book

Language revision	**Prohibition**

16 Bungled burglaries
Students' Book

Learner training	Reading: self-assessment/text types
Reading/Speaking	Jigsaw reading: crime stories
Vocabulary	Phrasal verbs
Language focus	**Past simple/Past continuous**
Writing	Crime story

Activity Book

Listening	Crime anecdote
Language practice	**Past simple/Past continuous**
Pronunciation	Regular past tense endings

Module 6: Music

36 Roots
Students' Book

Reading	Styles of music
Speaking/Listening	Music quiz/Opinions about music
Function focus	Expressing likes and dislikes

Activity Book

Language practice	**Likes and dislikes**
Pronunciation	Word stress

37 A pop star
Students' Book

Speaking	Pop star survey
Reading	Magazine article: interview
Language focus	**Reported questions**
Writing	Music project: inventing a pop group

Activity Book

Listening	Top five
Language practice	**Reported questions**

38 Making an album
Students' Book

Speaking	Music survey
Listening	Interview/Pop song
Language focus	**Gerunds and infinitives**
Writing	Music project: album cover

Activity Book

Language practice	**Gerunds/infinitives**
Reading	Karen's Story (1)

39 On stage
Students' Book

Reading	Magazine article: *On tour*
Function focus	Making informal arrangements
Pronunciation	Intonation/Sounds: /w/ /k/ /g/
Writing	Music project: concert review

Activity Book

Language practice	**Suggestions**
Language revision	**Adverbs of frequency**

40 The violin virtuoso
Students' Book

Listening	Classical music extracts
Reading	Life story of Paganini
Language focus	**Adverbs**

Activity Book

Language practice	**Adverbs**
Reading	Karen's Story (2)

41 Fluency
Students' Book

Learner training	Listening to pop songs/Body language
Listening/Speaking	Dialogue/Roleplay
Pronunciation	Word stress
Writing	Music project: interview/display

Activity Book

Listening	Music extracts

42 Revision
Students' Book

Language practice	(From the module)
Vocabulary	Word building
Learner training	Parts of speech/Module check
Language revision	**Test yourself**

Activity Book

Language revision	**Test yourself**
Pronunciation	Silent letters

Module 7: Health

43 The painful past
Students' Book

Reading	History of medicine
Language focus	*Have/get something done*

Activity Book

Listening	Medical records
Language practice	*Have/get something done*

44 The dark side of the sun
Students' Book

Speaking/Listening	Holiday dangers
Reading	Health shop leaflet
Language focus	**Quantity**
Writing	Essay about sunbathing

Activity Book

Language practice	**Quantity**
Listening	Eating habits

45 At the doctor's
Students' Book

Reading	Magazine article: *Chinese medicine*
Listening	Doctor's appointment
Function focus	Going to the doctor's/Roleplay
Pronunciation	Consonant clusters

Activity Book

Language revision	*Some/any/no/every*

46 A doctor and a half
Students' Book

Reading	Magazine article: *Island doctor*
Listening	Telephone conversation
Function focus	Advice and instructions/Roleplay
Writing	Sentences using linking words

Activity Book

Language practice	**Instructions/Advice**
Listening	Dialogue

47 Harder than Everest
Students' Book

Speaking	Problems of disabled people
Reading	Magazine article: disabled climbing
Language focus	**Future perfect**
Pronunciation	Contractions

Activity Book

Listening	Radio programme
Language practice	**Future perfect**

48 Fluency
Students' Book

Listening	Phone-in programme
Learner training	Telephone strategies/Evaluating writing/Pronunciation problems
Speaking	Roleplays: phone-in/doctor
Reading/Writing	Letter giving advice

Activity Book

Listening	Fortune Squares
Pronunciation	Homophones

49 Revision
Students' Book

Language practice	(From the module)
Pronunciation	Phonetic crossword
Language revision	**Test yourself**
Learner training	Revising vocabulary/Module check

Activity Book

Language revision	**Test yourself**

LEARNING TO LEARN

A Organise your learning

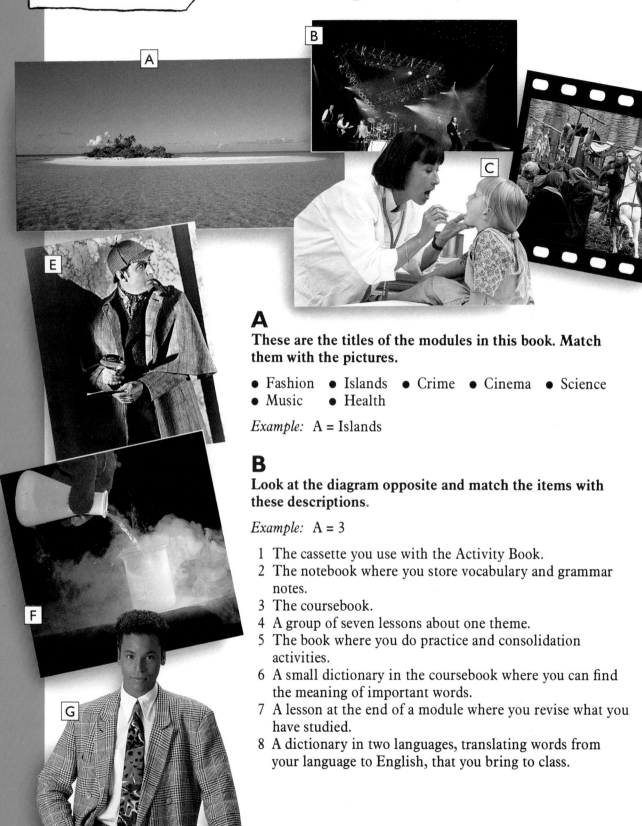

A

These are the titles of the modules in this book. Match them with the pictures.

- Fashion
- Islands
- Crime
- Cinema
- Science
- Music
- Health

Example: A = Islands

B

Look at the diagram opposite and match the items with these descriptions.

Example: A = 3

1. The cassette you use with the Activity Book.
2. The notebook where you store vocabulary and grammar notes.
3. The coursebook.
4. A group of seven lessons about one theme.
5. The book where you do practice and consolidation activities.
6. A small dictionary in the coursebook where you can find the meaning of important words.
7. A lesson at the end of a module where you revise what you have studied.
8. A dictionary in two languages, translating words from your language to English, that you bring to class.

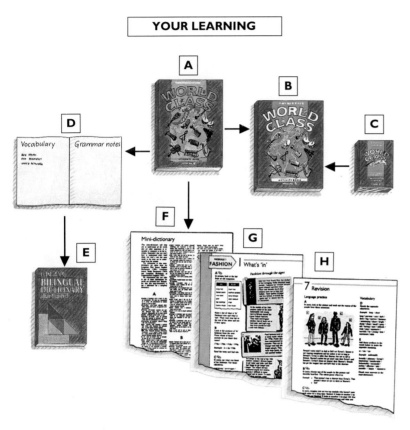

YOUR LEARNING

C

In pairs, work out five questions to ask about the Students' Book.

Examples: Which word comes after *burglar* in the mini-dictionary?
What page is Lesson 32 on?

Now ask and answer the questions with another pair.

D

In pairs, interview your partner and find out which of these classroom activities he/she likes doing.

- listening to the cassette
- working in groups
- speaking to your partner
- reading
- speaking games
- listening to stories
- writing letters/stories
- acting out situations

- tests
- projects/grammar games
- pronunciation exercises
- crosswords/puzzles
- grammar exercises
- vocabulary exercises
- 'test yourself' activities

E

Match the tenses with the sentences in the box below.

Example: 1 e)

1 Future *going to*
2 Present simple
3 Past simple
4 Future *will*
5 Present perfect
6 Present continuous

---

a) I've been to London twice.
b) Liverpool will win the cup.
c) She's watching TV.
d) Once upon a time there was a young princess.
e) I'm going to study French next year.
f) I get up at eight o'clock.

Now look at the Language section in the Module check (page 107). Evaluate yourself for the tenses using the scale provided.

Example:
Future *going to* = 3
(I sometimes have problems with it.)

F

In the grammar section of your notebook, write other examples of these tenses. Write translations of the examples in your own language.

B Understanding English

A

In pairs, read this advice about listening. Decide if it is good or bad.

Example: 1 = good

1 Before listening, you should think about what you are going to hear.
2 When you look at the questions, you should try to predict the answers.
3 The first time you listen, you should try to understand everything.
4 The first time you listen, you should try to get the general idea.
5 Stop listening if you do not understand everything.
6 If you have problems, ask your teacher to play the tape again.
7 You should use your dictionary while listening.

B 📼

Look at the pictures of Linda and Mohammed. Guess how old they are and what language(s) they are studying. Then listen and find out.

Linda

Mohammed

C 📼

Copy the table, then listen again and complete it.

	Linda	Mohammed
Hours a week	*two*	
Years studied		
Problems		
Use outside the class		

D

How much of each interview did you understand? Look at the graphs in the Module check on page 107. Copy and complete the graphs for the first and second time you listened to each of the interviews.

E

In pairs, interview your partner about his/her English.

Example: A: How many hours a week do you study English?
B: I do five hours of English a week.

F

Look at the mini-dictionary extract and match the parts which are numbered with the words below.

Example: 1 = example sentence

spelling / definition / example sentence / grammatical form / pronunciation / stress

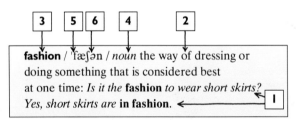

| 3 | 5 | 6 | 4 | 2 |

fashion / ˈfæʃən / *noun* the way of dressing or doing something that is considered best at one time: *Is it the **fashion** to wear short skirts?*
*Yes, short skirts are **in fashion**.* ← | 1 |

Did you know?

English has taken many words from other languages: *police* is from French, *hamster* from German, *democracy* from Greek and *cafeteria* from Spanish.

G

Dictrio game. In pairs, read the definitions from the mini-dictionary in the box below. Guess one of the words. Then check your answer in the mini-dictionary and you'll find the other two words.

Example: c) = *heat* (looking in the mini-dictionary the other words = *heart* / *hearse*)

1 a) a car which is used to carry a body in a coffin to the funeral
   b) the part of your body in your chest that pumps the blood round the body
   c) the feeling of something hot

2 a) a person who breaks into buildings to steal things
   b) to set on fire
   c) to put a dead person into the ground

3 a) the colour made by mixing red and white
   b) a robber of ships
   c) a part of a field on which games are played

4 a) (a person) with light-coloured hair, . . .
   b) the red liquid that flows round the body
   c) a loose garment for women, reaching from the neck to about the waist

H

Organise your vocabulary book. Write down important words from this lesson and include:

- spelling
- part of speech (noun/verb, etc.)
- meaning (definition or translation in your language)
- example sentence(s)

Write the information, like this:

Crime: noun – something that is wrong and that can be punished by the law:
Killing people is a crime.

5

C Speaking and writing

A

Look at the pictures and say which are problems for you when you are speaking English.

Nina Ghizikis from Greece

 B

I speak very slowly, because I don't think in English. I have to translate everything.

Brahim Lareki from Morocco

C

I often get stuck when I'm speaking, because I don't know a particular word in English.

A Often, when I see a new word, I don't know how to pronounce it.

Pia Posio from Italy

Diego Valdano from Argentina

B

Match the problems in exercise A with this advice.

1 If you don't know a word in English you don't have to stop speaking. Either think of a word that you know which is similar, e.g. *car* instead of *lorry*. Or explain it in a few words, e.g. *It's like a big car that you can carry things in.*
2 Don't try to translate your thoughts exactly; try to use the English you know.
3 Remember that your English classes are often the only opportunity you get to practise your English, so don't worry about feeling silly.
4 You can find out the pronunciation of new words in your dictionary by looking at the phonetic symbols. You can also find out the stress of new words.

 D

I feel silly speaking English with my partner in class. I prefer speaking in Spanish.

C

Think of two example sentences for each of the speaking situations below.

Example: a) = I really love swimming.

a) talking about your likes/dislikes
b) telling stories
c) asking for personal information

Pronunciation

D

Look at the phonetic chart on page 113. Use the symbols to identify the following words and write them down.

Example: 1 = science

1 /ˈsaɪəns/ 2 / ˈsɪnəmə/
3 / helθ/ 4 /ˈmjuːzɪk/
5 /ˈfæʃən/ 6 /kraɪm/
7 /ˈaɪləndz/

The symbol ' marks the stress. Mark the stressed syllable in each word. Then listen to the words and check your answers.

☐
Example: 1 science

E

Phonetic bingo. Copy the bingo card frame. Fill it in with your own choice of phonetic symbols and example words, like this:

/əʊ/ (g<u>o</u>)	/t/ (<u>t</u>o)	/e/ (b<u>e</u>d)
/s/ (<u>s</u>ee)	/aɪ/ (m<u>y</u>)	/k/ (<u>c</u>an)
/uː/ (t<u>w</u>o)	/h/ (<u>h</u>ow)	/ɔː/ (f<u>ou</u>r)

Cut up a sheet of paper into nine square pieces. Then listen to the sounds on the cassette. If you have got the sound on your bingo card, cover it up. When you have covered all the squares, shout 'Bingo'.

F

Read the note below. Correct five mistakes in it.

Example: 1 sister = sisters

> To: Ms Tomasini   Date: 23rd September
>
> I am sixteen and I have two sister and one brother. I really like swim and I go swimming every day. When I leave school I want to go university and study to be a doctor.
> I think English is important for work. If you are a doctor you have speak and understand some English. When we study English I like speaking in class, especially when we discuss things. The biggest problem for me is listening, and I often don't understand the casette.

G

Now write a short note to your teacher, talking about yourself and your English.

Stage 1 Use the network below to plan what you are going to write.
Stage 2 Use your plan to write the note (as in exercise F).
Stage 3 Check your note for mistakes and then give it to your partner to check.
Stage 4 Write a final version of the note.

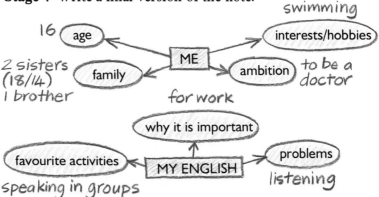

A

In groups, look at the list from an old magazine.

In	Out
long hair	short hair
flared jeans	leather jackets
mini-skirts	long dresses
pink	dark colours
big earrings	rings
heavy music	rap music

Make a list of what is 'in' (fashion) *now* and what is 'out'. Then read your list to the rest of the class and see if they agree.

B

Look at the pictures of 'in' fashions from the past. From which of these periods do you think they come?

1750s / 1790s / 1920s / 1970s

Example: A = the 1920s

Read the texts and find out.

C

In pairs, say what you think of the fashions. Use these adjectives.

interesting / extravagant / silly / uncomfortable / nice / horrible / weird / shocking /

Example:
'I think the fashion in picture A is strange but interesting.'

Fashion through the ages

A

After the First World War, the clothes of the swinging 1920s shocked many people. Fashions for women became more relaxed and freer than before.
5 Their hair became much shorter and dresses were not as long and wide as before. Their clothes became brighter and less formal, to match the new music and 'in' dances like the
10 Charleston.

B

In the middle of the 18th century, some of the most fashionable rich young men in Britain copied the
5 latest Italian fashions. They wore extravagant clothes, lots of make-up to look pale, and high wigs that were powdered and
10 tied with ribbons.

C

Punk fashions were as aggressive as punk music, which arrived in the 1970s. Punks chose the least conventional hairstyles
5 possible. They cut their hair in strange ways and often dyed it bright colours. They usually wore large boots, torn jeans and painted leather jackets.

D

In Europe at the end of the 18th century, women's dresses began to get wider and wider and their hair began to get longer and
5 longer. The widest dresses measured nearly two metres, making it difficult to move around and sit down. To make themselves prettier, some
10 women had enormous hairstyles. These were often decorated with flowers, feathers and even fruit!

Language focus: COMPARISON

D

Look through the texts and find examples of the rules in the box.

Example: 1 a) = Their clothes became brighter . . . (A, line 7)

> 1 To compare two things we use comparative adjectives.
>   a) For short adjectives add *-er*. (*nicer*)
>   b) For adjectives ending in *-y* change to *-ier*. (*sillier*)
>   c) For long adjectives add *more* or *less*. (*more/less comfortable*)
>   d) Before comparatives we can use *much* for emphasis. (*much nicer*)
>   e) After comparatives we often use *than*. (*A is nicer than B.*)
>
> 2 To compare two things we can also use *as* + adjective + *as*.
>   a) To say that things are equal we use *as . . . as*. (*as long as*)
>   b) To say things are different we use *not as . . . as*. (*not as weird as*)
>
> 3 To compare three or more things we use superlative adjectives:
>   a) For short adjectives add *-est* or change to *-iest*. (*the nicest / the prettiest*)
>   b) For long adjectives add *most* or *least*. (*the most /least comfortable*)

E

In pairs, spot the differences between Victor and his twin brother, Keith. Then write sentences about them.

Examples: hair: Victor's hair is longer than Keith's.
Keith's hair is not as long as Victor's.

Victor

Keith

F

Write five sentences about the physical similarities between Victor and Keith using these words.

dark / tall / thin / big nose / long legs / round head

Example:
Victor is as dark as Keith.

G

In pairs, take turns to make statements and answer true or false about the pictures in exercise B.

Example:
A: In the 1920s dresses were longer than before.
B: False.

Fashion project

H

Find an old photo of your parents or grandparents. Write a description of their clothes.

9

2 Looking good

A

Label the clothes in the picture using these words.

jeans / shirt / dress / jacket / skirt / belt / zip / collar / trousers / buttons / pocket / sleeve

B

In pairs, discuss what you think of the clothes in the picture.

Example: A: I think the leather jacket is nice.
           B: I think his shirt is horrible.

Report some of your opinions to the rest of the class.

Example: We think the leather jacket is nice but the shirt is horrible.

C

Does the boy buy the jacket in the picture? Does the girl buy the skirt? Listen to the dialogues and find out.

Function focus: BUYING CLOTHES

D

Listen again to the shop assistant and two customers. Then complete the sentences below.

SHOP ASSISTANT	CUSTOMERS

From dialogue 1

SHOP ASSISTANT	CUSTOMERS
1. . . . . I help you?	No, thanks. I'm just 2. . . . .
	How much is this?
It's 3. . . . . pounds.	That's too 4. . . . .
5. . . . . about this one?	No, I don't like the 6. . . . .
	It's not 7. . . . . enough.
That really suits you.	All right. I'll 8. . . . . it.

From dialogue 2

SHOP ASSISTANT	CUSTOMERS
Can I 9. . . . . you?	I'm 10. . . . . for a skirt.
What 11. . . . . are you?	I don't know. Can you measure me?
Would you like to try 12. . . . . on?	
	Where are the changing 13. . . . . ?
They're over there.	It's too 14. . . . .

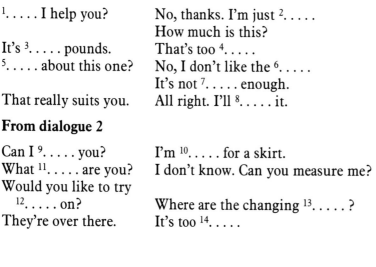

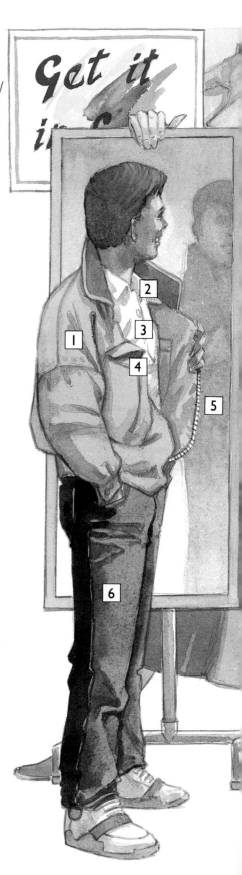

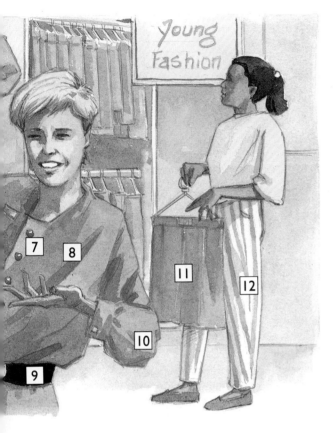

F LEARN TO LEARN

Complete the text about shopping with the verbs below in the correct tense. Use the mini-dictionary to help you.

Example: try on
First find the verb = *try*
Then look for the different meaning with *on* = *try on*

try on = to put on clothes to see if they fit

try on / go with / put on / look for / think of

I'm a terrible shopper. Last month I went shopping. I was [1] . . . . a new jersey to [2] . . . . my new jeans. In the first shop I saw a red and yellow jersey and I [3] . . . . it . . . . Then I bought it. When I got home I [4] . . . . the jersey and asked my family: 'What do you [5] . . . . it?'

Pronunciation

G 📼

Listen to these two vowel sounds.

Group 1	*Group 2*
/ə/ trousers	/ɪ/ jacket

Listen and put the words below into the correct group according to the sounds.

mea*su*re / pain*ted* / coll*ar* / leath*er* / music / short*er* / pock*et* / col*our* / wom*en* / decora*ted* / fre*er* / pretti*er* / dress*es* / copi*ed* / *e*nough / *a*ggressive / *e*normous / *a*rrive / w*o*men

Listen again and repeat the words.

Fashion project

H ✏️

Design your own jacket. Draw a picture of it and write a description. Think of these things:

- size
- colours
- materials
- pockets
- zips
- sleeves
- collar

E 🥾

In pairs, take turns to buy something. Use the cues to help you.

SHOP ASSISTANT   CUSTOMER

- Ask if you can help → Say what you're looking for
- Ask about size ⇄ Give your size
- Show clothes ⇄ Say why you don't like it /them
- Suggest something else ↘ Ask about price
- Give the price ⇄ Ask to try it /them on
- Say where the changing room is → Say you want to buy it /them

3 A megamodel

A

Look at the picture of Naomi Campbell. Try to guess the answer to these questions.

1 Is she a successful model?
2 What are her other interests outside modelling?
3 Does she plan to marry and have children?

Now read the text and find out.

Fashion Superstar

Heads turn and I look round to see what is happening. Naomi Campbell has just come into the office. She is dressed casually, wearing jeans and a T-shirt, but there is
5 something special about her. Wherever Naomi goes she is the centre of attention.

She is one of a small group of international fashion stars, who are today's 'megamodels'. They jet around the world,
10 make more than $10,000 a show, and are as famous as Hollywood actors and rock superstars.

Naomi has already been on the front cover of the most important fashion
15 magazines like *Vogue* and she has become the most successful black model since Iman in the early 1980s. But she knows that the working life of a top model is short. As well as modelling, Naomi has recently started
20 a career in music, singing with the group Vanilla Ice. She also knows many people in the world of cinema, including ex-boyfriend Robert de Niro. However, she has not done any acting yet.

25 Naomi has certainly come a long way since an agent saw her looking at a shop window in London, when she was fifteen. But she still remembers where she comes from, and she still has not forgotten how
30 hard her mother worked for her education after her father had disappeared when she was a baby.

There are plenty of parties and fun in her life and Naomi likes the glamour of the
35 world of fashion. But she also hopes one day to marry and have a family. And she wants to find a man who loves her for the right reasons, not someone who is in love with her image.

B

Read the text again and decide if these statements are true or false.

1 Megamodels make an enormous amount of money.
2 Naomi has already appeared on the front cover of *Vogue*.
3 She has recently appeared in a film.
4 She started modelling when she was a child.
5 She doesn't want her future husband only to love her image.

Language focus:

JUST, RECENTLY, STILL, YET, ALREADY

C

Match the rules with the examples.

Examples	Rules
1 She **still** remembers where she comes from. (line 28)	a) This shows that something has happened (sooner than expected).
2 Naomi has **already** been on the front cover of . . . magazines (line 13)	b) This shows that an action happened a moment ago.
3 She has not done any acting **yet**. (line 24)	c) This shows that something has happened in the last few weeks/months.
4 Naomi has **recently** started a career in music. (line 19)	d) This shows that an action or situation is continuing.
5 Naomi Campbell has **just** come into the office. (line 2)	e) This shows something that hasn't happened but it probably will.

Find an example in the text of *still* with the present perfect.

D

Complete the report about Karl using these words. Some are used more than once.

just / recently / still / yet / already

It's early on Monday morning at a top male modelling office in London. Karl has ¹. . . . . arrived and is ². . . . . a bit sleepy. He is tall, blond and looks brown, because he has been on holiday in Ibiza ³. . . . .

At twenty-four Karl is young for a male model, but he has ⁴. . . . . appeared in several important magazines, though he has not been on TV ⁵. . . . . Although it is difficult for many models to find work at the moment, Karl has been very busy ⁶. . . . . and his future looks bright.

He ⁷. . . . . keeps in contact with his friends and family in his native Sweden, and ⁸. . . . . goes back there as often as he can. He has not got any plans to marry ⁹. . . . . , though he has ¹⁰. . . . . met an Italian girl who he is very much in love with. 'She's great!' Karl says, suddenly showing interest.

E

Write five sentences about your life, using these words.

just / recently / still / yet / already

Example:
I have *just* finished a history project.

F

In pairs, ask your partner questions about his/her life.

Examples:
A: Have you been to the cinema recently?
B: No, I haven't.
A: Have you done your maths homework yet?
B: Yes, I have.

Fashion project

G

List the advantages and disadvantages of being a model.

Examples:
advantages – travelling
disadvantages – a lot of work

4 Dressed to kill

A
Look at the pictures and match the animals with the things. Then say how you feel about them.

Example: 1 (crocodile) and D (shoes of crocodile skin)

B
In pairs, make a list of which animals we kill for fashion. Say why.

Example: We kill crocodiles to make shoes.

C
Listen to a radio interview with Dr Gurney.

1 List four animals he mentions.
2 How are these four animals used in the fashion industry?

Language focus:

PRESENT SIMPLE / PRESENT CONTINUOUS

D

Listen again to Dr Gurney. Then complete the sentences in the box.

> 1 People always . . . . . to look good.
> 2 We . . . . . thousands of animals every year for tests.
> 3 We . . . . . whales for their oil.
> 4 African elephants . . . . . fast.
> 5 Crocodiles sometimes . . . . . great cruelty.
> 6 More and more people . . . . . cruelty-free products.

E

Look at the completed sentences in exercise D. Complete the rules, a and b, with the correct tenses.

present simple / present continuous

a) The . . . . . tense describes a fact, or something that always happens.
b) The . . . . . tense describes something happening now.

Now look at the verbs below. In English we can never, or rarely, use them in the continuous. Can you use any of them in the continuous in your language?

want / love / hate / know / need / understand / remember / belong / think / realise / hear / see / matter

F

Use the cues to write the questionnaire, using the present simple or present continuous.

Example: 1 Do you think it is important to protect animals?

Are YOU a friend of animals?

1 think / important / protect animals / ?
2 know / which of these animals / endangered species / ?
   a) rhino b) cow c) Arctic fox d) rabbit e) leopard
3 at the moment / wear / any of these things / ?
   a) leather b) fur c) ivory
4 ever / wear / any of the things in item 3 / ?
5 usually / buy / cruelty-free shampoo and soap / ?
6 ever / buy / products made from endangered animals / ?

G

In pairs, use your questionnaire to interview your partner. Is he/she a friend of animals?

Pronunciation

H

Listen and repeat these words. Be careful how you pronounce the sounds at the beginning of the words.

1 blue, black, brown, bright
2 please, play, product, prepare, pretty
3 shampoo, shop, shirt, skirt, skin
4 start, still, strange, sleepy, slow

Add other words to the lists if you can.

Fashion project

I

Add clothes and other products to the lists below.

Animal friendly
soap made from vegetable oils

Cruel to animals
soap made from whale oils

15

5 Appearances matter

A
In pairs, discuss these questions.

1 How much does the appearance of another person influence you?
   a) not at all   b) a bit   c) a lot
2 Are you careful about your appearance?
   a) never   b) sometimes   c) always

B
Read the poem and text. Who do you identify with most?

Alfie / Alfie's teachers / Buddy / Buddy's dad

BUDDY'S DAD

Buddy thought he was going to die when his dad came downstairs ready to go at six thirty. He was dressed in his complete Teddy Boy
5 outfit – drainpipe trousers, jacket with velvet collar, bootlace tie, thick crepe-soled shoes and fluorescent green socks. His hair was slicked back with oil and it was obvious
10 that he'd taken great care to look as tidy as possible. He'd dressed himself in his 'best' for the occasion.
   Buddy felt sick. The evening was
15 going to be a disaster.
   "Dad," he said weakly.
   "What?"
   "Can't you put something else on?"
   "Why?"
20 "Well, it's just . . . Mr Normington . . . won't like it."
   "He'll 'ave to lump it then, won't he?" There was defiance in his dad's voice.

from *Buddy* by Nigel Hinton

ALFIE

My brother Alfie's had
his hair cut like a hedge,
it sticks up in the middle
and it's spiky round the edge.

5 He brushes it each morning
and keeps it fairly clean,
you'll see him when he's coming,
he's dyed it bottle green.

Now Alfie thinks he's trendy
10 he thinks he's really cool
looking like a football pitch
as he walks to school.

All the teachers hate him
because he's got green hair,
15 and other kids they laugh at him
but Alfie doesn't care.

by *David Harmer*

C
Read the poem and text again and answer these questions.

1 What is unusual about Alfie's appearance?
2 How do other people react to Alfie's appearance?
3 What is Alfie's attitude?
4 How does Buddy feel about his dad's clothes?
5 Who do you think Mr Normington is?
6 What is the attitude of Buddy's dad?

D
Add words from the poem and text to these lists. Then add other words of your own if you can.

Adjectives describing hair: spiky
Adjectives describing general appearance: trendy
Clothes: trousers

Function focus: DESCRIBING PEOPLE

E

Match the questions and answers.

1 What does she like?	a) A T-shirt, jeans and a pair of trainers.
2 What does she usually wear?	b) She's cheerful and independent. She doesn't care what people think about her.
3 What does she look like?	c) Pop music, reading and horses.
4 What is she like?	d) She's small and thin, with long blonde hair and blue eyes.

F

Write questions to go with the notes below about Pedro.

1 **Looks:** *young* / medium height / *round* face / *straight*, short *brown* hair / *dark* complexion
2 **Clothes:** *smart* / jacket and trousers
3 **Personality:** *calm* / *efficient*
4 **Interests:** *modern art*

Example: 1 What does he look like?

G

Now make notes about Greta. Use these words to replace the words in *italics* in exercise F.

blonde / casual / nervous / square / middle-aged / curly / detective stories / pale / T-shirt / disorganised / jeans

Example: **Looks:** middle-aged / medium-height / square face

H

In groups, each student thinks of a famous person or someone everyone knows. Take turns to ask questions and then guess who it is.

Fashion project

I

Write a description of someone you know well.

Stage 1 Make notes like those in exercise F.
Stage 2 Use the notes to write a description.
Stage 3 Display your description, including a photograph if possible.

Did you know?

Men in fifteenth-century Europe wore shoes with very long points. Sometimes they were so long that they were tied at the knee.

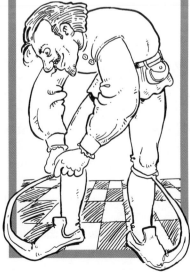

6 Fluency

A

Look at the pictures, then listen to the story of Cinderella. When the storyteller pauses, correct the mistakes that she has made.

Example: 1 Cinderella was poor. She didn't wear mini-skirts and leather jackets. She wore very old clothes.

B [LEARN TO LEARN]

If you are shopping in an English-speaking country, which of the following things should you do?

1 If you don't know a word, say it in your own language.
2 Speak as fast as possible.
3 If you don't know a word, try to explain it with other words.
4 Use your hands and facial expressions to help you communicate.
5 Look at the shop assistant when you are speaking.
6 If you make a mistake, stop and repeat the sentence.
7 If you make a mistake, don't worry, just continue.
8 Before you go into the shop, prepare what you're going to say.

C

In pairs, take turns to be a clothes shop assistant and a difficult customer who disagrees with all suggestions about material, colour, style, etc. See how long you can continue.

Example: A: I'm looking for a jacket.
B: This leather one's nice.
A: No, I don't like leather.
B: What about this cotton one?
A: No, it's too short.

Pronunciation

D 🔊

Listen and notice how we link words with the sounds /j/, /w/ and /r/.

1 They'll be ^{/j/}extinct soon.

2 That's too ^{/w/}expensive!

3 Animals go blind or ^{/r/}even die.

Listen again and repeat the sentences.

E

Read Nigel's letter of complaint. Which of these does he mention?

- the colour has faded
- the zip broke
- there are holes in them
- it shrank when I washed it

|1| 53 Arbuckle Street, Doncaster

|2| 24th June

|3| Dear Sir/Madam,

|4| I am writting ~~ to you about a pair of 'Wonderworld' trainers I bouht ~~ last month from Supersports in Doncaster. ~~ I have only played

|5| futball ~~ in them twice, but their are already three or four holes in the bottom of one shoe. I took the shoes back to Supersports but ~~ the manager of the shopp was very unpleasant, and refused to ~~ refund my money.

|6| I enclose the receipt ~~ for £25 and would be grateful if you would refund ~~ my money.

|7| Yours faithfully,

|8| Nigel Graves

F 🔲 LEARN TO LEARN

Evaluate Nigel's letter for presentation. Grade it from 1–5, like this:

> 5 = excellent
> 4 = good
> 3 = satisfactory
> 2 = bad
> 1 = terrible

Find six spelling mistakes in the letter and correct them.

G

Match the numbers on the letter with the words below.

Example: 1 = address

signature / start to letter / paragraph about reasons for writing / address / paragraph asking for refund / paragraph giving details about the complaint / ending / date

Fashion project

H

Write a letter of complaint to a clothes company about a jersey you bought.

Stage 1 Write notes about:
the jersey / problems with it / what action to take

Stage 2 Use the notes to write the letter with three paragraphs.

Stage 3 Give the letter to your partner to check.

Stage 4 Write your final version of the letter.

I 🖊️

In pairs, collect everything you have done for your fashion project. Organise it as a magazine or poster and display it in the classroom.

7 Revision

Language practice

A

In pairs, look at the picture and work out the names of the people from these sentences.

Brenda's jeans aren't as dark as Seb's or Kevin's. Sharon is not wearing sunglasses and her jacket is not as long as Brenda's. Kevin is taller than Sharon, but not as tall as Brenda. Sharon's jacket has got more zips than Kevin's and Brenda's. Kevin's shoes are cleaner than Sharon's. Brenda has got the longest hair and Seb's hair is the shortest.

B

In pairs, choose one of the people in the picture and describe him/her. The others guess who it is.

Example: A: This person's hair is shorter than Kevin's. This person's shoes are not as dirty as Sharon's.
B: Seb!

C

In pairs, imagine you are two top models who haven't seen each other for a long time. Student A looks at number 1 on page 108 and Student B looks at number 1 on page 110. Use the cues to talk about where you have been and what you have done.

Example: A: Where have you been recently?
B: I've just come back from New York.

Vocabulary

D

Match the opposite adjectives.

Example: long – short

long / nervous / tiny / dark / dirty / big / narrow / fantastic / interesting / short / bright / cheap / clean / small / nasty / old / boring / easy / difficult / wide / nice / expensive / horrible / fat / young / thin / enormous / calm

E

Add these prefixes to the words below to make the opposite meaning.

in- / im- / un-

Example: unfriendly

friendly / pleasant / formal / dependent / comfortable / fashionable / successful / perfect / efficient / tidy / possible / happy / expensive

Check your answers in the mini-dictionary.

Test yourself

F
Complete these sentences.

1 The (warm) . . . . . clothes are those worn by the Inuit people, who have to survive in the Arctic.
2 Sarongs from Bali are not (long) . . . . . Japanese kimonos.
3 Scottish kilts are (colourful) . . . . . other British men's clothes.
4 The (good) . . . . . clothes for the desert are long robes.
5 Traditional Mexican hats are (large) . . . . . than American cowboy hats.

G
Complete the conversation between Tarquin and Marc with these words.

just / recently / still / yet / already

TARQUIN: Hi, Marc. Where have you been ¹. . . . .?

MARC: I've ². . . . . got back from Tokyo. I'm ³. . . . . feeling a bit tired.

TARQUIN: Yeah? I haven't been there ⁴. . . . ., but I'm going next month. I've been very busy. This month I've ⁵. . . . . done three big shows and I've got another one tomorrow.

MARC: And where's Antonio been ⁶. . . . .?

TARQUIN: He's ⁷. . . . . gone to Paris. I think he went this morning. What about Terry?

MARC: Well, he's ⁸. . . . . in San Francisco. He ⁹. . . . . hasn't finished that film, you know the one about dolphins.

TARQUIN: Look Marc, I've got to go. I'm late for a meeting with my agent. And I haven't had breakfast ¹⁰. . . . .!

MARC: OK. Bye! See you soon.

H
Choose the correct form of the verb.

1 He *listens* / *is listening* to the news every day.
2 She *loves* / *is loving* bright clothes.
3 I'm sorry, I *don't understand* / *am not understanding*.
4 Paul *has* / *is having* a shower.
5 I *think* / *am thinking* it's horrible.

I
Do the Module check on page 107.

Do the Module check on page 107.

Language check

COMPARISON

Short adjectives
Dresses became **shorter than** before.
Men in Britain copied **the latest** Italian fashions.

Long adjectives
Fashions . . . became **more relaxed than** before.
Punks chose the **least conventional** hairstyles.

as . . . as
Punk fashions were **as aggressive as** punk music.
Dresses were **not as long as** before.

JUST, RECENTLY, STILL, YET, ALREADY

She **still** remembers where she comes from.
She **still** has not forgotten how hard her mother worked.
She hasn't done any acting **yet**.
Naomi has **already** been on the front cover of *Vogue*.
She has **just** come into the office.
She has **recently** started a career in music.

PRESENT SIMPLE / PRESENT CONTINUOUS

People always **want** to look good.
We **are killing** thousands of animals every year.
Crocodiles sometimes **suffer** great cruelty.
More people **are buying** cruelty-free products.

8 Island holidays

A

In pairs, say in which of the continents the islands below are situated.

America (North and South)	Asia	Europe
The Galapagos (Ecuador)	Honshu (Japan)	Skye (Scotland)

The Galapagos / Honshu / Skye / Cyprus / Cuba / Sri Lanka / Bali / Crete / Barbados / Jamaica / Borneo / Ireland / Sicily / The Bahamas / Ibiza / Singapore / Greenland

Add to the list of islands if you can. Which island would *you* like to visit?

B

Which of the headings in the table below do you think are important when going on holiday? Read the brochure about Barbados. Copy and complete the table with information from the brochure.

Beaches	30 miles / white sand
Weather	
Sports	
Places to visit	
People	
Hotels	
Food	

C

Listen to the dialogue and check the information with the brochure. Write down five mistakes that the new travel agent makes.

Example: 1 Travel agent: it's always very hot
Brochure: fresh island breezes keep us cool

B A R

BADOS

Welcome to beautiful Barbados where the sun shines for over 3,000 hours a year, and where we have fresh island breezes to keep us cool. We have more
5 than thirty miles of white sandy beaches and clear blue waters. In Barbados you can relax and forget the stress and worries of the rest of the world.

There is lots to do for everyone. There are
10 ideal conditions for swimming on the west coast, and for windsurfing and surfing on the south coast. There are also many interesting places to visit on the island and excursions to go on, like the cruise on the
15 famous pirate ship, the *Jolly Roger*.

The Barbadian people are friendly, fun-loving and hospitable. We have a distinctive culture, with African roots and an important British influence. We can also be
20 proud of our country, which has a literacy rate of over 95% and over 350 years of democratic government.

There is a wide choice of hotel accommodation, from luxury hotels to
25 modest, comfortable guest houses for you to stay in. And you must try some of our fantastic food, with such exotic delicacies as lobster and flying fish to choose from.

Function focus:

ASKING FOR HOLIDAY INFORMATION

D

Listen again to the travel agent and customer. Then complete the questions.

> 1 Could you . . .?
> 2 How can you . . .?
> 3 How much . . .?
> 4 What's the weather/food . . .?
> 5 What are the beaches/people . . .?
> 6 What is there . . .?

E

In pairs, choose a holiday destination (real or imaginary). Think of adjectives to persuade others that your choice is the best place to visit. Write notes using the headings in exercise B, like this:

Crete
Beaches: fantastic / sandy
Weather: beautiful – warm and sunny from May to October
People: very friendly / a lot of people speak English
Food: delicious traditional Greek dishes

F

In groups, ask and answer about your holiday places.

Example: A: What's the weather like in Crete?
B: It's absolutely lovely for most of the year. From May to October it's always very warm and sunny.

Now decide which place you want to visit. Report to the rest of the class the most popular holiday place in your group.

9 Exploring Barbados

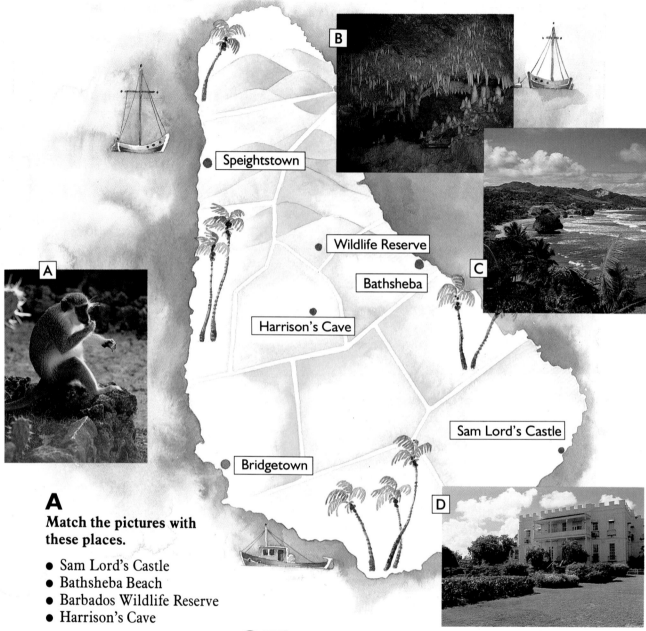

Speightstown

Wildlife Reserve

Bathsheba

Harrison's Cave

Sam Lord's Castle

Bridgetown

A

B

C

D

A
Match the pictures with these places.

- Sam Lord's Castle
- Bathsheba Beach
- Barbados Wildlife Reserve
- Harrison's Cave

B
Listen to the conversation between two tourists and a tour guide. Look at the places on the map and write them down in the order you hear them.

Example: 1 Bridgetown

C
Listen again and answer these questions.

1 What can you see at Speightstown?
2 What are the most interesting animals at the wildlife reserve?
3 How long does the tour of the cave take?
4 What country does the area around Bathsheba look like?
5 When was Sam Lord's Castle built?
6 Where is the treasure supposed to be buried?

Language focus:

PREPOSITION REVIEW

D

Listen again to the conversation in exercise B and complete the directions with these prepositions.

with / on / on / at / up / for / in / down / into / across / out of / of / of / along / through / next to / from / back /

Take the main road and go ¹. . . . . Bridgetown. Go ². . . . . Bridgetown and then go ³. . . . . the coast. You will see beautiful beaches ⁴. . . . . the road. If you are interested ⁵. . . . . old buildings, you can visit the old forts in Speightstown.

When you drive ⁶. . . . . Speightstown you'll go ⁷. . . . . a hill. As you come ⁸. . . . . it, you'll see the wildlife reserve ⁹. . . . . the left. If you are keen ¹⁰. . . . . wildlife it's really worth visiting. ¹¹. . . . . the wildlife reserve go along the Bridgetown road until you arrive ¹². . . . . Harrison's Cave. Don't be frightened ¹³. . . . . visiting it, there are tours with guides. The cave is famous ¹⁴. . . . . its beautiful stalactites.

Then you can go ¹⁵. . . . . the island to Bathsheba. If you're bored ¹⁶. . . . . sightseeing you can go to the beach. On your way ¹⁷. . . . . to the hotel and if you're fond ¹⁸. . . . . romantic places, you can visit Sam Lord's Castle.

E

List six examples of each of the following in the text above. Add other examples to the two lists if you can.

- verbs with prepositions
- adjectives with prepositions

Examples: Verbs: go into
Adjectives: fond of

Pronunciation

F

Listen to the sentences and mark the stressed words.

Example: 1 Go through the town and turn
left next to the football ground.

1 Go through the town and turn left next to the football ground.
2 You go up the hill and you'll see the house on the right.
3 Go along the Bridgetown road until you arrive at the cave.
4 Go under the bridge and the castle is opposite the church.
5 Go past the cinema and it's the third on the right.

In pairs, practise saying the sentences with the correct stress.

G

In pairs, think of an interesting place to visit in your area.

Examples: a historic building / a beach / a nature reserve

Write about the place and how to get there, like this:

> If you are interested in castles, you can visit Ludlow which is near Leominster. Go out of the town and take the Shrewsbury road. After twelve kilometres you will see a turning for Ludlow on the left. Go into the centre of the town and you will see the castle, next to the river. The castle is very large and from the top of it you can see for miles.

H

In groups, read out your suggestions.
Decide on the most popular place to visit.

10 Life on Skye

A

In pairs, look at the photo of Kirsty McDonald and the picture of Skye. Guess things about her life. Talk about:

where she lives / her family / her hobbies and interests

B

Read Kirsty's letter to Ana in Fortaleza, Brazil. Find out if the things you guessed were correct. Then answer these questions.

1 What has Ana been doing recently?
2 Why is the island of Skye cut off?
3 How many books has Kirsty read this term?
4 What project has she been doing?
5 How many songs has she learnt?
6 Why are Kirsty's parents tired?

C

Match these topics with the paragraphs in the letter.

● the weather
● finishing the letter
● Ana's letter
● Kirsty's homework
● other news

D

Find words or expressions that link different pieces of Kirsty's news.

Example: It's *also* been raining.

Berneray Farm,
Isle of Skye,
Scotland

3rd February

Dear Ana,

1   Thanks very much for your letter and the photo. I'm glad that you've been having a good holiday.

2   Life is very different here. We're in the middle of winter and it's been raining for weeks, so I'm a bit depressed. As well as that, we're cut off from the mainland at the moment! The sea has been rough, so the ferry has not been working since the weekend.

3   I've been busy recently and I've been studying a lot. I've read three English books so far this term. On top of that I've been doing a really big geography project. I've been reading about Brazil and it sounds like a fantastic place!

4   As well as studying, I've been practising the guitar a lot. I've learnt a couple of songs, but I'm still not very good! I've also been helping Mum and Dad on the farm. They're getting pretty tired because they haven't been getting much sleep. This time of year is when the lambs are born, so sometimes they have to stay up all night.

5   Well, I must stop now and get back to my homework. I hope you are getting on all right at your new school. Write soon and tell me about it.

Best wishes,
Kirsty

Language focus: PRESENT PERFECT SIMPLE / PRESENT PERFECT CONTINUOUS

E
Look at the example sentences in the box.

> **Present perfect continuous**
> a) This tense describes an activity with a result in the present:
> *They're pretty tired because they **haven't been getting** much sleep.*
> b) It also describes an activity that started in the past and is continuing:
> *I**'ve been doing** a geography project all about South America.*
>
> **Present perfect simple**
> c) This tense describes something that has been completed:
> *I**'ve read** three books so far this term.*

Are the sentences below like a, b or c?

1 I've learnt a couple of songs.
2 It's also been raining for weeks, so I'm a bit depressed.
3 As well as studying, I've been practising the guitar a lot.

F
Put the verbs in brackets in the present perfect simple or present perfect continuous.

1 How many books (you/read) . . . . . this year?
2 She is very tired now because she (work) . . . . . a lot.
3 How long (you/learn) . . . . . English?
4 He (just finish) . . . . . that letter.
5 They (play) . . . . . tennis since six o'clock.

G
In pairs, act out conversations using the topics below.

Example: A: What have you been doing?
B: I've been writing a letter.
A: How much have you written?
B: I've written ten lines.

- write a letter (lines)
- read a book (pages)
- do homework (pages)
- make models (five)
- do a history project (pages)
- draw pictures (two)

H
In pairs, imagine you meet an old friend who you haven't seen for a long time. Find out and give news about what has happened and what you have been doing.

Example:
A: What have you been doing?
B: Well, I've been very busy. I've been playing a lot of football. I've played in the school team twice!

I
Write a letter to a friend giving your news.

Stage 1 List the things you have been doing recently and the things you have finished.

Stage 2 Use your list to write a paragraph plan.
1 starting the letter
2 your news
3 more news
4 finishing the letter

Stage 3 Use your plan to write the letter. Think about where to put the address and date (look at Kirsty's letter).

11 Lord of the Flies

A

**In pairs, discuss picture A.
Use the questions below.**

Example:
A: Where do you think it is?
B: I think it's in Africa.

1 Where do you think it is?
2 What is the weather like
there?
3 Is it inhabited?
4 Would you like to go there
on holiday?
5 What would you do there?

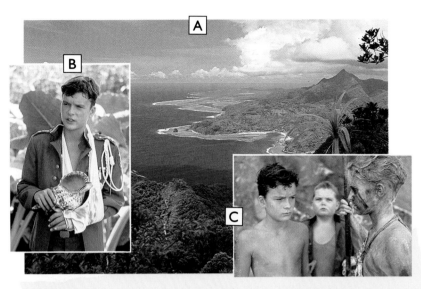

B

**Read the three extracts from
Lord of the Flies, about a
group of schoolboys whose
plane crashed on the island.
Answer these questions.**

1 What do the boys decide to
find out?
2 Which boys go on the
expedition?
3 Are there any people on
the island?
4 How do the boys feel?

Extract 1

Ralph smiled and held up the conch for silence.
'Listen everybody. I've got to have time to think things out.
I can't decide what to do straight off. If this isn't an island
we might be rescued straight away. So we've got to decide if
this is an island. Everybody must stay round here and wait
and not go away. Three of us – if we take more we'd get all
mixed and lose each other – three of us will go on an
expedition and find out. I'll go, and Jack, and, and . . .' He
looked round the circle of eager faces. There was no lack of
boys to choose from.
'And Simon.'

Extract 2

'There's no village smoke, and no boats,' said Ralph wisely.
'We'll make sure later; but I think it's uninhabited.'
'We'll get food,' cried Jack. 'Hunt. Catch things . . . until
they fetch us.'

Extract 3

Ralph spread his arms.
'All ours.'
They laughed and tumbled and shouted on the mountain.
'I'm hungry.'
When Simon mentioned his hunger the others became
aware of theirs.
'Come on,' said Ralph. 'We've found out what we wanted to
know.'

C

Listen to three dialogues. Match them with a, b and c.

a) two people imagining a situation like that in *Lord of the Flies*
b) an expert talking about survival
c) a group of people on the island

Language focus:

CONDITIONALS REVIEW

D

Listen to the dialogues in exercise C again and complete the sentences.

First conditional: 'If we . . . . . a fire, somebody . . . . . see us.'
Zero conditional: 'If they . . . . . the food, it . . . . . much safer.'
Second conditional: 'If I . . . . . in that situation, I . . . . . make a hut.'

E

Copy and complete the table with the tenses used for conditionals.

	Condition	Consequence
First	*if* + present simple	. . . . .
Zero	*if* + ...	. . . . .
Second	*if* + ...	conditional (**would**)

Which conditional do we use to talk about:

a) 'unreal' or unlikely situations – situations that are imagined and probably will not happen?
b) general information and rules?
c) 'real' situations – things that might happen?

F

Look at the situations below. Complete the suggestions by putting the verbs in brackets in the correct tense.

Example: 1 'If we *build* a boat, we *will be able to* escape.'

1 You are on a desert island: 'If we (build) . . . . . a boat, we (be able to) . . . . . escape.'
2 You are at home with your family: 'If we (live) . . . . . on a desert island, I (go) . . . . . swimming every day.'
3 A doctor is talking: 'If people (eat) . . . . . too much fruit, they usually (have) . . . . . stomach problems.'
4 You are at school, talking to a friend: 'If we (be) . . . . . on a desert island, we (not have to) . . . . . do our English homework!'
5 You are on a desert island: 'I think this is the best place for the hut. If we (build) . . . . . it here, we (be) . . . . . near the river.'
6 An ecologist is talking: 'Wild pigs are not aggressive animals. They (be) . . . . . only dangerous if people (attack) . . . . . them.'

Did you know?

Lord of the Flies is by Nobel Prize-winner William Golding. It is about a group of British schoolboys marooned on a deserted island.

12 Island survival

1 plastic sheet
2 hooks
3 penknife
4 axe
5 box of matches
6 tropical plants book
7 first-aid kit
8 fishing line
9 garden fork
10 vegetable seeds
11 mirror
12 cooking pan
13 nails
14 gun

coconuts
island
D
H
jungle
beach
F

A

Imagine you have to spend a long time alone on a desert island. In pairs, choose eight of the above objects to take with you. Explain why.

Example: A: I'd take the hooks, because then I'd be able to fish.

B: I'd take the garden fork, because . . .

B

Listen to two teenagers discussing survival on the island. Match these things with the letters on the map.

the huts / the fire / the vegetable garden / the boat / the store

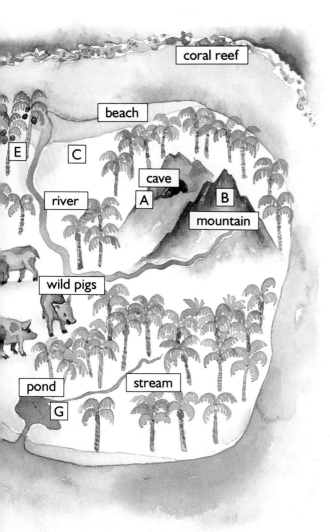

coral reef

beach

E

C

cave

river

A

B

mountain

wild pigs

pond

G

stream

Function focus:

AGREEING AND DISAGREEING

C

Which of these expressions from the dialogue is used to agree and which is used to disagree?

I don't agree. / So do I. / You're right./
I wouldn't do that. / I agree. / I think so too. /
That's a good idea. / I don't think so. /
I'm not sure. / OK. / So'd I. / All right. /
I think you're wrong.

Pronunciation

D 📼

Listen and say how the people disagree.

Examples: 1 I don't agree. = strong (very certain)

2 I don't agree. = hesitant (uncertain)

In pairs, practise the expressions of disagreement in exercise C with strong or hesitant intonation.

E

In groups, plan where you would put things on the island. Remember to use the language and intonation for agreeing and disagreeing.

Example: A: I would put the huts next to the cave.

B: I wouldn't do that, because it's a long way from the river. I think we should put them next to the fire.

C: I don't agree. I'd build them next to the river.

Copy the map of the island and draw the things on it.

F 🗣

Report your plans to the rest of the class. Decide which group has the best plan.

G 📼

Listen and find out what happened to the boys in *Lord of the Flies*.

1 How did they start the fire?
2 What did the boys eat?
3 What frightening thing did they see in the trees?
4 Who did the 'hunters' kill?
5 What happened in the end?

31

13 Fluency

A

Listen to the radio programme. Which of these books do Mark and Lucy decide to take to a desert island?

- a book about tropical plants
- *Lord of the Flies* by William Golding
- *An Unsuitable Job for a Woman* by P.D. James
- *Buddy* by Nigel Hinton
- a collection of detective stories
- *Robinson Crusoe* by Daniel Defoe
- a collection of poems

B [LEARN TO LEARN]

Listen again. Match these accents with the three people.

Australian / British / American

1 the presenter
2 the girl
3 the boy

Which accent is the easiest for you to understand? Which is the most difficult?

C

You have a CD player and a video player to take with you to a desert island. Make a list of two books, two CDs and two video tapes to take with them.

Examples: books: *Robinson Crusoe* / an Agatha Christie novel
records: *Over the Edge* by Dwayne Benefit / *Heartbroken* by Delma
videos: *The Addams Family* / *Terminator 2*

In groups, find out what the others would take.

D

Look at the picture of a Barbadian mansion and listen to the directions. Where in the garden is the treasure buried?

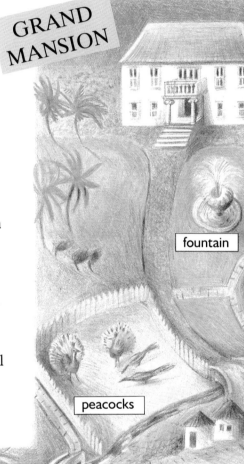

GRAND MANSION

fountain

peacocks

stream

swimming pool

beach

E

E 🔊
Listen again. Which of these expressions does the person listening use to show that she is following the directions?

OK. / Sorry. / I agree. / Yes. / Excuse me? / I see. / Right.

car park

vegetables

cave

pond

cave

summerhouse

path

tennis court

café

F 🗨
In pairs, look at the picture again.

Student A Choose a place in the garden to hide some treasure and give directions to it.

Student B Listen to the directions (showing attention with words from exercise E).

Find the place where your partner has hidden the treasure.

G ✎ 📖 LEARN TO LEARN
Write a description of an island.

Stage 1 Draw an island (look at the drawing in Lesson 12 to help you).

Stage 2 Write notes about the island like these:
1 *Size/geographical features:* two kilometres long / one kilometre wide / a big hill at one end / flat land at the other end / a stream
2 *Climate/vegetation:* hot and tropical / lots of rain / thick jungle in most of island / coconut palms near beach
3 *Wildlife:* monkeys and wild pigs in the jungle / lots of different birds: peacocks/parrots.
4 *People:* small village with a port / two hundred people

Stage 3 Use your notes to write four paragraphs about the island.

Stage 4 Give your island description to your partner. He/She looks for mistakes and signals them like this:
T = tenses ←WO→ = word order P = punctuation
S = spelling V = vocabulary Pr = prepositions

Stage 5 Your partner also evaluates your description, like this:
A = really interesting and well-written
B = interesting with some mistakes
C = not very interesting and with quite a lot of mistakes

Stage 6 Rewrite your description, correcting the mistakes.

Did you know?

Islands can appear and disappear. In 1963 the volcanic island of Surtsey, near Iceland, was formed. It was called after the Icelandic god of fire.

14 Revision

Language practice

A

In pairs, look at the picture. Write six sentences about what the man has been doing since he arrived on the island.

Examples:
He has been writing a diary.
He has built a hut.

B

Conditional game. Write five conditional sentences.

Example:
If it rains, I will stay at home.

In pairs, take turns to read out half of one of the sentences. The other person has five guesses to finish it. The person who guesses the most sentences wins.

Example:
A: If it rains, . . .
B: . . . I will stay at home.

Vocabulary

C

Make the adjectives below into nouns, by taking away or changing the endings in *italics*. Use the mini-dictionary to help you.

lucky / windy / sunny /
noisy / comfortable /
fashionable / beautiful /
careful / colourful /
romantic / democratic /
fantastic / mysterious /
dangerous / disastrous

D

Match the examples of *get* with the definitions. Use the mini-dictionary to help you.

1 How can you *get* there?
2 I hope you are *getting on* all right.
3 Mum and Dad *got* me one for Christmas.
4 He has *got* two brothers.
5 I must *get back* to my homework.
6 If insects bite people they *get* malaria.

a) to advance or go well
b) to obtain or buy
c) to catch an illness
d) to return to
e) to arrive
f) to have or possess

Pronunciation

E

Listen to these three vowel sounds.

Group 1	*Group 2*	*Group 3*
/aɪ/ island	/iː/ breeze	/ɪ/ interesting

Listen and put the words into the correct group according to the sounds. Then listen again and repeat the words.

Test yourself

F

Complete the story of Robinson Crusoe with these prepositions.

back / across / up / under / into / from / into / at / along / to

Robinson Crusoe was a sailor from Britain whose ship sank. He swam ¹. . . . . the coast of a small, deserted island. The first night he was frightened, so he climbed ². . . . . to the top of a tree to sleep. In the next few days he rescued some important things ³. . . . . the ship, which was near the coast.

After that he put up his tent ⁴. . . . . a big rock. Then he explored the island. He walked ⁵. . . . the coast and also went ⁶. . . . . the jungle. Next he went ⁷. . . . . the island to the other side.

While he was on the island he did lots of things. He built a house, collected fruit and hunted wild goats. He also made a canoe, but he couldn't get it ⁸. . . . . the water. In the end a ship stopped ⁹. . . . . the island and took him ¹⁰. . . . . to Britain.

G

Put the verbs in the correct tenses in the diary.

H
Do the Module check on page 107.

Language check

PREPOSITIONS

Prepositions with verbs
Go **along** the coast.

Prepositions with adjectives
I am bored **with** all those old buildings.

PRESENT PERFECT SIMPLE / PRESENT PERFECT CONTINUOUS

I'm a bit **depressed**, because it**'s been raining** for weeks.
I**'ve been exploring** the island today.
I**'ve been practising** since Christmas.
I**'ve learnt** a couple of songs.

CONDITIONALS

First conditional
If we **make** a fire, somebody **will** see us.

Zero conditional
If people **eat** too much fruit, they **are** ill.

Second conditional
If we **had** a fishing line, we **could** catch fish.

1659

<u>October 21st</u>
Today I (explore)¹_____ the island, but I still haven't finished. I (find)²_____ a good place to put my tent.

<u>November 2nd</u>
Now I (bring)³_____ the last useful things from the ships. Also, I am very tired because I (work)⁴_____ very hard.

<u>November 17th</u>
I (finish)⁵_____ making a cave behind my tent. If I (have)⁶_____ a spade, I (can)⁷_____ do it much quicker.

<u>December 20th</u>
I finally (move)⁸_____ all of my things into the cave. Everything is very wet, because it (rain)⁹_____ for days. If the rain continues, I (not be able to)¹⁰_____ get enough food.

35

A

Read the newspaper reports. Use the mini-dictionary to check any difficult words. Then match the reports with these crimes.

- shoplifting • smuggling
- dangerous driving

One of the stories is false. Which one do you think it is?

B

Read the reports again. Write **T** (true), **F** (false) or **DK** (don't know).

1. It is illegal to drive a milk float at more than thirty miles an hour.
2. Mr Sprinkle crashed the milk float.
3. The police arrested Sabina for shoplifting.
4. It was difficult for the detectives to catch Henry Smith.
5. You can't take animals into Britain.
6. Mrs Arbuthnot bit the customs officer.

A

Constable George Wilkins said: 'I saw Mr James Sprinkle driving a milk float dangerously down Cambourne Hill. Several drivers 5 had to pull over to avoid him. At first I could not keep up with him. But when the milk float got to the bottom of the hill, I jumped off my bicycle, and tried to arrest him. He 10 shouted: "I will not stop. I am mad for speed!" But soon after that, he crashed into the back of Mr Arthur Jenkin's hearse.'

B

During her interview, Ms Sabina Firm said: 'It is my fault. I told Henry I would leave him if he did not get me a colour television. So he went out and came back 5 with one. At that moment, the police came in and arrested Henry for shoplifting. One of the detectives said they caught him quickly because he has his name, Henry Smith, tattooed on his 10 forehead. He had taken a taxi and told the driver: "You have seen nothing – OK? You have not seen Henry Smith."'

C

Mrs Angela Arbuthnot was charged at Dover court with two serious offences: trying to smuggle animals into Britain, and 5 assaulting a customs officer. Mr Reginald Hobhouse, the customs officer, told the court: 'When I was looking through Mrs Arbuthnot's suitcase, I saw two 10 pet hamsters. When I tried to pick one of them up, it bit me and Mrs Arbuthnot shouted: "You mustn't touch Ronny, he's very sensitive." Next, she hit me over the head 15 with her handbag.'

C

Complete the sentences with these verbs.

pull over / keep up with / look through / come back

1 She ran very fast and I couldn't . . . . . her.
2 At the airport the customs officer took my bag and . . . . . it.
3 He went out to buy some bread but he didn't . . . . .
4 He was driving dangerously, so the policeman asked him to . . . . .

Function focus: PROHIBITION

D

Which of the three sentences describe laws and which describes what a person thinks it is important *not* to do?

a) It is *illegal to drive* a milk float at more than thirty miles an hour.
b) You *can't take* animals into Britain.
c) You *mustn't* touch Ronny!

E

In pairs, say which of the things below are illegal for young people (under 16) in your country. Then write five sentences about them.

- drive a car
- ride a bicycle
- buy alcohol
- buy cigarettes
- take drugs
- work
- leave home
- ride a small motorbike
- fly an aeroplane
- vote in an election
- go to a casino
- eat chewing gum
- go to discotheques

Example: It is illegal to drive a car before you are seventeen.

F

In pairs, look at the words below which are all crimes. Use the mini-dictionary to find out their meaning.

murder / burglary / shoplifting / smuggling / bank robbery / mugging

Which are the most serious of these crimes? Put them in order.

G

In groups, read about four crimes and say which they are from the list in exercise F. Put them in order of seriousness.

1 Susan has five small children and very little money. She stole food from a supermarket.
2 Samantha is a professional burglar. She stole a lot of silver from the house of a rich family.
3 Eric needed a lot of money for a medical operation for his mother. He robbed a bank to get it.
4 Mr Smith smuggled his pet dog into Britain.

Did you know?

In Waterloo, Nebraska, it is illegal for a barber to eat onions between the hours of 7a.m. and 7p.m.

16 Bungled burglaries

A
[LEARN TO LEARN]

In pairs, look through the previous lessons in this book. In which lessons have you seen the types of text in the list below? Put them in order of difficulty.

Example:
newspaper article = Lesson 15

- newspaper article
- magazine article
- tourist brochure
- poem
- extract from a novel
- letter
- extracts from a history book

B

Look at the texts about two burglars. Which of the following do they come from?

a novel / a local newspaper / a book of true stories / a magazine

C

Work in pairs. Student A reads text A. Student B reads text B. Find out about your partner's story by asking these questions.

1 How did the burglar get into the house?
2 Did he find anything valuable?
3 What happened next?
4 Why was he caught by the police?

When you have finished, read the other story yourself.

A

What a laugh!

Jan Tomisc's career as a burglar was not going very well. One night, as he was walking through the streets of Warsaw, Jan saw a large house and decided to break into it. He got in through an unlocked window but, while he was filling his
5 sack with silver, he heard voices. He quickly hid behind the sofa and a moment later two men came into the room.
'Right let's hear it.' said the first man.
'All right.' replied the second. Jan immediately recognised the voice of one of the men. It was Jaraslav, one of Poland's
10 greatest comics, who imitated famous people.
Jaraslav began imitating the prime minister and Jan, who was hiding behind the sofa, started laughing to himself. Next, Jaraslav imitated the Bishop of Cracow. Jan started to shake with laughter and tears were running down his face. In the
15 end Jan exploded with laughter. Jaraslav immediately broke off his performance and rang up the police. Jan was still laughing when the police came to arrest him.

B

HUNGRY HOUSEBREAKER

William Brady of Hove was convicted of burglary at Brighton magistrates court last Thursday, and sentenced to six
5 months in prison. Brady broke into one of the large houses in Lansdowne Avenue. He got in through the kitchen window, but was disappointed to find
10 the door to the rest of the house locked.

He did not find anything valuable in the kitchen, but he did find a cupboard full of
15 food. First he had a large pork pie, then he ate a ham sandwich, followed by a chicken sandwich. He finished off with an enormous piece of choco-
20 late cake.

After that, he relaxed in his chair and soon dropped off. He was still sleeping happily when the police came to arrest
25 him the next morning.

Language focus:

PAST SIMPLE / PAST CONTINUOUS

E

Look at these examples from text A.

Jan Tomisc's career . . . *was not going* very well. (line 1)
As he *was walking* through the streets of Warsaw, Jan *saw*
a large house. (lines 2 and 3)

Which tense, past simple or past continuous, is used:

a) to describe the situation at the beginning?
b) to describe the background situations or longer actions in
   the story?
c) to describe the shorter actions in the story that 'interrupt'
   the longer actions?

F

Complete these sentences from text A.

1 While he . . . . . his sack with silver, he . . . . . voices.
2 Jan, who . . . . . behind the sofa, ... laughing to himself.
3 Jan was still . . . . . when the police . . . . . to arrest him.

**Look through the two texts and decide which of the words
below link sentences. Then write down the linking words
that introduce the past continuous and those that introduce
the past simple.**

one night / as / through / while / a moment later / right / next /
in the end / immediately / one of / first / then / after that /
soon / when

G

**In pairs, use these notes to write a short newspaper article,
using some of the linking words in exercise F.**

Example: Inspector Jardin was a Paris detective. *One night* he
got a call about a burglary at a big mansion. *When*
he arrived . . .

Inspector Jardin / Paris detective / got call about burglary /
big mansion / arrived at big mansion / owner waiting / lots of
silver missing / going into dining room / saw book lying on
floor / Jardin picked it up / he read 'This book belongs to
Marcel Grauf, 24 Rue Antoine Paris' / Jardin drove to address /
getting there / saw Grauf / coming home / carrying bag with
silver

D

**Match these verbs from
the texts with the
definitions in the box
below.**

Example: 1 c)

1 break into (A, line 3)
2 drop off (B, line 22)
3 break off (A, line 15)
4 ring up (A, line 16)

a) stop doing something
b) telephone
c) use force to get into a
   building
d) fall asleep

17 Detectives

A

In pairs, unjumble the letters to find the names of three famous detectives:

1 sisM Mrpale
2 hSerlcko Hmoles
3 Pliihp Moweral

Can you think of any other famous detectives from films, television or books? Report them to the class.

B

Look at the picture of Cordelia Gray, a detective from the book *An Unsuitable Job for a Woman* by P.D. James. Guess the answers to these questions.

1 Why is she not a 'typical' detective?
2 Where do you think she is in the picture?
3 What do you think has recently happened?

Now read the extracts from the book and find out.

C

Read the extracts again and answer these questions.

1 How did Cordelia know that the boy had been a tidy person?
2 What things had the boy left untidy before he died?
3 What other things were strange?
4 What does Cordelia begin to suspect?

She had examined the cottage in accordance with the Super's instructions. What did she now know about the dead boy? What had she seen? What could she deduce?

5 He had been almost obsessively neat and tidy. His garden tools were wiped after use and carefully put away, his kitchen had been painted and was clean and ordered. Yet he had abandoned his digging less than two feet from the end of a row;
10 had left the uncleaned fork in the earth; had dropped his gardening shoes casually at the back door. He had apparently burnt all his papers before killing himself, yet he had left his coffee mug unwashed. He had made himself a stew for
15 his supper which he hadn't touched. . . .

But suppose someone had visited him that evening. . . .

But suppose it wasn't Mark who had wished to conceal the fact that visitor had called that night;
20 suppose it wasn't Mark who had washed and put away the second mug; suppose it was the visitor who had wished to conceal the fact of his presence. . . .

A word dancing at the back of Cordelia's mind,
25 an amorphous half-formed jangle of letters, came suddenly into focus and, for the first time, spelt out clearly the blood-stained word. Murder.

Language focus: PAST PERFECT

D

List five things that **Mark** had done before he died.

Example: He had stopped digging before the end of the row.

E

Look at the diagram and answer the question below.

past		present	future
+	×	×	
↑	↑	↑	
He had stopped digging before the end of the row. (*past perfect*)	MARK'S DEATH	Cordelia looking for clues	WILL SHE SOLVE THE MURDER?

In which situation do we use the past perfect, a, b or c?

a) to describe an activity at a specific time in the past
b) to describe an action in the past
c) to emphasise that one action in the past happened before something else in the past

F

Look at the picture of **Cordelia Gray's room**. Write five sentences about what you think the detective had done before she left the room.

Example: She had burnt some papers.

G

In groups, compare your sentences and work out a theory about what she had done before she left the room.

Example: First she had ...
Then she had ...
Next she had ...
After that, she had ...

One person from each group reports the theory to the rest of the class.

Did you know?

Allan Pinkerton became the first private detective when he opened the Pinkerton National Detective Agency in 1850 with this motto: 'We never sleep.'

18 Murder in Marbella

A 📼

Look at the people who were at a large mansion on the night of August 11th. Guess which of them was murdered. Listen to the story and find out.

Jimmy Capaldi

Susan Capaldi

Brigite Muller

Madame Lebrun

Jimmy Capaldi Jr

Arthur Williams

Stephanie Capaldi

Christos Popodopolis

B 📼

Listen again to the story. Write down the nationality of the people and identify their relationship with the dead person.

business partner / butler / personal physician / daughter / wife / son / biographer / cook / personal secretary / daughter's boyfriend

Example: Bruce Maxwell: Australian / business partner

Lady Julia Hamilton

Jaime Peñafiel

Bruce Maxwell

Language focus: MODALS FOR SPECULATION

C

Listen and complete the sentences with these modals.

couldn't / must / may / could / might / can't

> 1 Susan Capaldi . . . . . be the murderer. She was his wife.
>
> 2 Stephanie Capaldi loved her father. She . . . . . be the one who did it.
>
> 3 Brigite Muller . . . . . have killed him, but why? She was only his secretary.
>
> 4 Williams . . . . . know who the killer is. Butlers always know what is happening.
>
> 5 Bruce Maxwell . . . . . have shot him. But what motive did he have?
>
> 6 I think Jimmy Capaldi Jr . . . . . have done it because he wanted his father's money.

Look at the completed sentences. Match the modals with the descriptions.

1 must   a) weak possibility
2 may   b) impossibility
3 could / might   c) certainty
4 can't / could't   d) possibility

Which sentences in the box speculate about the present and which speculate about something that has happened?

D

Write sentences about the story using the cues below.

Example: Lady Julia Hamilton couldn't have killed Capaldi.

1 Lady Julia Hamilton / couldn't / kill Capaldi
2 Now / Susan Capaldi / must / feel / sad
3 Dr Popodopolis / could / murder / Capaldi
4 Madame Lebrun / may / know / who / killer
5 Jaime Peñafiel / might / shoot / Capaldi

E

Look at the information about the characters on page 112. Write five sentences speculating about who the murderer is and why he/she did it.

Example:
It could be Stephanie. She could have killed her father because she wanted to marry Jaime, and her father tried to stop her.

F 🗫

In groups, discuss your ideas and agree on a theory about the murder. Report your theory to the class.

Pronunciation

G

Listen again to some sentences from the story. Write down the words which are emphasised.

Example: couldn't

19 Alibis

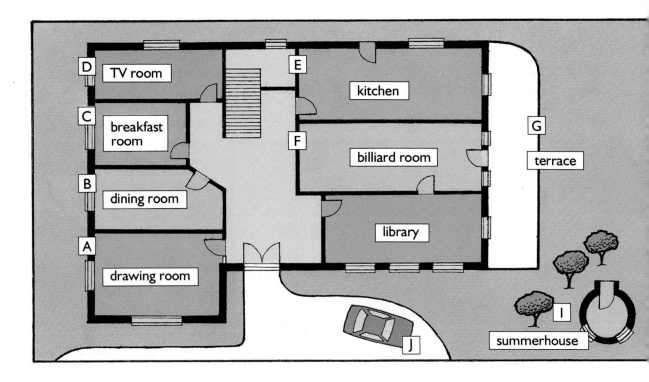

A 📼

Look at the plan of the Capaldi's mansion. Listen to Inspector Garcia checking the statements of four of the people. Match the names with the places on the plan. Which places could the murderer have come from?

Example: A = Susan Capaldi

B 📼

Listen again to the statements. Which of these words do the people use when they are hesitating and can't think of anything to say?

That's right / Er . . . / Please / Mmm / Well / Of course not / You know / Yes / Actually

C 📼

Listen once more and find what is wrong with these statements.

Example:
Susan Capaldi wasn't reading a book, she was writing a letter.

> **Susan Capaldi: Statement**
> I was in the drawing room reading a book. I could hear the butler next door opening bottles until about 9.15. Then at about 9.25 I heard someone in the hall. Then at 9.30 I heard the shot.
> *S.Capaldi*

> **Dr Christos Popodopolis: Statement**
> I was fishing at the pond. At about 9.25 I saw a woman in the library. Then I heard the shot.
> *C.Popodopolis*

> **Brigite Muller: Statement**
> I was watching a tennis match on TV. I didn't hear anything.
> *B.Muller*

> **Bruce Maxwell: Statement**
> I was cleaning my car. It i[s] a lovely old Rolls and I never let anyone else touc[h] it. At 9.15 I saw a tall person in the library with Mr Capaldi.
> *B.Maxwell*

44

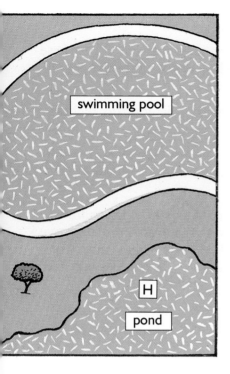

swimming pool

H

pond

Function focus:

CHECKING INFORMATION / QUESTION TAGS

D

Listen to the question tags and complete these questions.

Example: 1 You were in the drawing room reading a book,
weren't you?

1 You were in the drawing room reading a book, ...?
2 You could hear the butler opening bottles until about
9.15, ...?
3 At 9.25 you heard someone in the hall, ...?
4 You were fishing at the pond, ...?
5 It was a woman, ...?
6 You didn't hear anything, ...?
7 You weren't watching TV, ...?

Pronunciation

E

Listen again. Which of the question tags:

a) checks a statement that seems true?
b) checks information that seems suspicious or incorrect?

Repeat the question tags.

F

**In pairs, check the other suspects' statements. They may
not be true. Write notes to help you find the killer. Student
A looks at number 2 on page 108. Student B looks at
number 2 on page 110.**

Example: 9.20 front door open / 9.25 somebody in hall /
9.30 shot

G

**Write down who the murderer is on a piece of paper. Put
your name on it and give it to your teacher.**

H

**Now listen to the confession of the murderer. Were you
right? What was the real motive for the murder?**

Did you know?

Interpol is an international
organisation which hunts
criminals all over the world.
The headquarters is in a quiet
suburb of Paris.

20 Fluency

A

Listen to the story of the Australian outlaw Ned Kelly. Was it fair that they hanged him?

B

Listen again and complete this information about Ned Kelly's life.

1855	●	[1]. . . . .
1870	●	In trouble with [2]. . . . .
1878	●	Ned shot and injured [3]. . . . .
1878	●	Formed gang with [4]. . . . .
1879	●	[5]. . . . . men joined the gang
1880 (June)	●	Captured town of Glenrowan. Police killed [6]. . . . . members of gang. Injured Ned in [7]. . . . .
1880 (End)	●	Hanged in Melbourne. Last words: 'Such is [8]. . . . .'

C

In groups, play a judging game. Write these words on small pieces of paper and put them on the desk face down.

mugger / burglar / murderer / bank robber / dangerous driver / shoplifter

Student A takes one of the pieces of paper and tells the story of what happened and why.

Example: *mugger*: 'I took fifty dollars from this very rich man. I did it because I had no money. My family were living in one small room and we . . .'

As judges, the others decide what should happen to him/her.

Example: two years in prison / a fine of $10,000

Then Student B takes a piece of paper and tells his/her story.

D ▭ LEARN TO LEARN

Listen to five sentences with mistakes and look at the correct sentences below. Use these abbreviations to classify the mistakes.

Pron (pronunciation) / G (grammar) / V (vocabulary)

1 Her parents are called Sonia and Scott.
2 She became a detective last year.
3 He works for the Miami police.
4 Last week she caught two burglars.
5 The burglars were not very happy.

Listen again. Think about how the mistakes affect the meaning. Which is the worst and which is the least important mistake?

46

E
LEARN TO LEARN

In pairs, discuss your answers to the questions below.

1 What do you do when you know that you have made a mistake?
   a) I stop speaking.
   b) I continue speaking normally.
   c) I try to correct it.
2 What do you do when you hear your partner make a very simple mistake?
   a) I do nothing.
   b) I correct it.
   c) I laugh at him/her.
3 Should your teacher correct your mistakes when you are speaking?
   a) Yes, all of them.
   b) Only the important ones.
   c) No, because I get nervous.

Pronunciation

F

Listen to five sentences and write them down. Listen again and mark the stressed words. Then mark all the examples of the sound /ə/.

Example: I was writing a letter to my

lawyers.

Listen again and repeat the sentences.

Did you know?

A burglar who had tried to get into the window of a supermarket, had found that it was too small. He took off his clothes and threw them into the shop, but still couldn't get through. He had to ask a passing policeman for help!

G

Look at the stories in Lessons 15 and 16 again. Write your story of a bank robbery.

Stage 1 Think about these things:
the bank robber(s) / the bank / the people in the bank / what happened in the bank / the escape

Stage 2 Write a detailed plan. Include three paragraphs with these things:
   1 *Situation:* what the bank robbers were doing at the start of the story / the street outside the bank / what the people in the bank were doing
   2 *What happened:* what the robbers did / what they took / what the reaction of the people was
   3 *What happened in the end:* if they escaped and how / what the police did / what happened to the stolen money

Stage 3 Write the story. Remember to use linking words like these:
first / then / after that / still / next / immediately / in the end

Stage 4 When you have finished, check the story for mistakes.

H
LEARN TO LEARN

Give your story to your partner to evaluate for presentation and interest. Use these scales to give marks.

Presentation	Interest
5 very clearly written and very tidy	5 a very exciting story
4 clear and tidy	4 interesting
3 reasonable handwriting	3 quite interesting
2 difficult to read	2 not very interesting
1 nearly impossible to read	1 boring

21 | Revision

Language practice

A

How did the burglar get into the house? Look at the drawing of the house for clues. Then write five sentences about your theory.

Example: He could have climbed over the wall.

burglar alarm

TV cameras

B

In pairs, make sentences using these tenses.

present simple / past simple / past continuous / past perfect

Example: A: I *come* to class every day.
B: I *came* here yesterday.
A: I *was coming* here when I saw her.
B: I did my homework after I *had come* to school today.

Vocabulary

C

Complete the following text by replacing the verbs in brackets with these verbs.

get away / get to / come back / put on / break into / look through

The burglar (arrived at) [1]..... the house and (entered violently) [2]..... by the back window. He was (checking) [3]..... the cupboards when the owner (returned) [4]..... The burglar (placed on his head) [5]..... a mask, but he didn't (escape) [6]..... because the police were waiting for him in the garden!

D

Match these words.

1 steal   a) a bank
2 rob   b) a house
3 mug   c) a cassette player
4 burgle   d) in a supermarket
5 shoplift   e) a person

Pronunciation

E

Listen to these two vowel sounds.

Group 1   Group 2
/ æ / drank   / ʌ / drunk

He *drank* the cup of tea.
He'd *drunk* the cup of tea.

Listen to five more sentences. Put the verbs into the correct group according to the sounds. Then listen again and repeat the sentences. Look through your vocabulary book and find five more words with each sound.

Test yourself

F

Complete the story below. Put the verbs in brackets into the correct tense (past simple / past continuous or past perfect).

Lord Macaulay, the famous historian, was on holiday in Rome. One evening, after he (have) [1] . . . . . an excellent meal, he (walk) [2] . . . . . near the Colosseum and (look) [3] . . . . . at the ruins. Suddenly a man (come) [4] . . . . . past him and (knock) [5] . . . . . against him. Soon after, Macaulay (find) [6] . . . . . that his watch was missing.

Macaulay immediately (run) [7] . . . . . after the man, who (walk) [8] . . . . . very fast. Because Macaulay (not speak) [9] . . . . . Italian he shouted in English and (take) [10] . . . . . the watch that the man (hold) [11] . . . . . in his hand. Macaulay then (return) [12] . . . . . to his hotel feeling well satisfied with himself.

When he (get) [13] . . . . . back to his hotel, the owner (say) [14] . . . . . to him: 'Excuse me, signor, I (find) [15] . . . . . your watch in the dining room after you (go) [16] . . . . . out.'

G

Complete the sentences about the story with these words.

must have (× 2) / might have / could have / couldn't have

Example: 1 The other man *must have* been very surprised.

1 The other man . . . . . been very surprised about what had happened.
2 The man . . . . . been a doctor in a hurry, going to visit a patient.
3 He . . . . . been a British tourist because he didn't understand Macaulay.
4 The man . . . . . gone to the police to report the incident, but he probably didn't.
5 Macaulay . . . . . taken the watch to the police because he was an honest man.

H

Do the Module check on page 107.

Do the Module check on page 107.

Language check

PAST SIMPLE / PAST CONTINUOUS

As he **was walking** through the streets of Warsaw, he **saw** a large house.
While he **was filling** his sack with silver, he **heard** voices.
Jan **was** still **laughing**, when the police **came** to arrest him.

PAST PERFECT

He **had been** almost obsessively neat and tidy.
He **hadn't finished** his digging.
Had somebody **killed** him?
He **hadn't touched** his supper.

MODALS FOR SPECULATION

About the present
Susan Capaldi **couldn't be** the murderer.
Williams **may know** who the killer is.
She **can't be** the one who did it.

About the past
She **couldn't have done** it.
Peñafiel **may have murdered** him.
Brigite Muller **might have killed** him.
Bruce Maxwell **could have shot** him.
Jimmy Capaldi Jr **must have done** it.

A ✍

Talk about the sort of films you like from this list.

- comedy
- suspense
- crime
- romantic
- science fiction
- horror
- historical
- westerns
- adventure

Examples:

A: I like *Home Alone*. It's a good comedy.

B: I like *Alien*. It's a good suspense and science-fiction film.

B

Look at three film reviews. What sort of films are they? Match the reviews with the pictures.

1 Arnold Schwarzenegger is back with *Terminator 2*, the most expensive film ever made, costing an incredible 88 million dollars. The story carries on from *Terminator*, another episode in the war between machines and people. This time Schwarzenegger is a goodie, a robot programmed to protect the young John Connor, the future leader of the rebels against the evil machines. His enemy is T1000, a more advanced and deadly robot. The story is a bit weak, but there are some brilliant special effects, especially the final fight between the two robots. Don't miss it!

3 This adaptation of the 1960s TV show is quite ridiculous and a lot of fun. Anjelica Houston is absolutely magnificent as the vampish Morticia, adored by the romantic Gomez, played by Raul Julia. Other characters in the zany family include the psychopathic Uncle Fester, the children Wednesday and Pugsley, and a hand called 'Thing'. If you want a good time and a good laugh, make sure you see *The Addams Family*.

2 This remake of an old favourite, is extremely well-directed by Kevin Reynolds. Perhaps the star of the show is not the hero Robin, but the evil Sheriff of Nottingham, brilliantly played by Alan Rickman. Kevin Costner's performance is unconvincing, when compared to the Robin Hoods of the past, such as the great Errol Flynn. However, the film is full of exciting adventure and is really enjoyable. It is definitely worth seeing.

C

Read the film reviews again and answer these questions. Use the mini-dictionary to check any difficult words.

1 When did *The Addams Family* first appear?
2 What part did Anjelica Houston play?
3 What part did Arnold Schwarzenegger play in *Terminator 2*?
4 Who was the best actor in *Robin Hood*?
5 What part did Kevin Costner play?

D

Are these adjectives from the reviews positive or negative? Use the mini-dictionary to check the meaning.

magnificent / weak / well-directed / brilliant / unconvincing / exciting / enjoyable

Example: magnificent = positive (good)

Function focus: RECOMMENDING

E

Complete these sentences from the reviews recommending the films.

> 1 Make sure . . .
> 2 Don't . . .
> 3 It is definitely . . .

F

In groups, each student writes a sentence recommending a film, on a piece of paper. Mix up the papers. Take turns to select a paper and read out the sentence. Guess who wrote it.

Example: A: *Batman Returns* is worth seeing.
B: I think Ana wrote that.

G

Write a short review of a film you have enjoyed recently.

Stage 1 Write notes about:
the kind of film / title of the film in English / what the story is about / leading actors / director / good things about the film / your recommendation
Stage 2 Use your notes to write the review. Try to include some adjectives from exercise D.

H

In groups, ask questions about the things below to find out about the others' films.

● title ● story ● actors ● recommendation

Example: A: What's it called?
B: It's called *White Fang* in English.
C: And what's it about?
B: It's about a half-wolf, half-dog. He's trained by an Indian and he's friendly. Then . . .

Cinema project

I

Show your film review to your partner, to check for mistakes. Then write a final version. Look for a picture from an old magazine or newspaper to go with the review.

Who said that?

'If I made *Cinderella*, the audience would immediately be looking for a dead body in the coach.'
(*Alfred Hitchcock, director*)

23 Child stars

A

In groups, talk about films you have seen starring children. Write down the names of the children. Compare your list with other groups.

Example: GROUP A: There was a young girl in *The Addams Family*. We think she was Christina Ricci.

B

Listen to an interview from a film programme and answer these questions.

1 Who spent Shirley Temple's money?
2 How do child actors today save the money they earn?
3 Why was Christina Ricci's part in *The Addams Family* so good for her?
4 How much did Macaulay Culkin get from the second *Home Alone* film?
5 How old was Tatum O'Neal when she won an Oscar?

Language focus:

THE THIRD CONDITIONAL

C

Listen to the second part of the interview again. Complete the sentences below with the correct form of the verb.

Example: If Macaulay Culkin *hadn't made* 'Home Alone', he *wouldn't have met* the President of the United States.

1 If Macaulay Culkin (make) ..... *Home Alone*, he (meet) ..... the President of the United States.
2 If he (become) ..... famous, he (be) ..... in a Michael Jackson video.
3 If he (be) ..... in *Home Alone*, he (star) ..... in *My Girl*.

Shirley Temple

Charlie Korsmo

D

Look at the completed sentences in exercise C. Copy and complete the table with these words.

have / past perfect / past participle

Condition	Consequence
If + ... ,	would + ... + ...

In which situation do we use the third conditional, a, b or c?

a) to talk about future possibility
b) to talk about things that didn't happen in the past
c) to talk about imaginary situations in the present

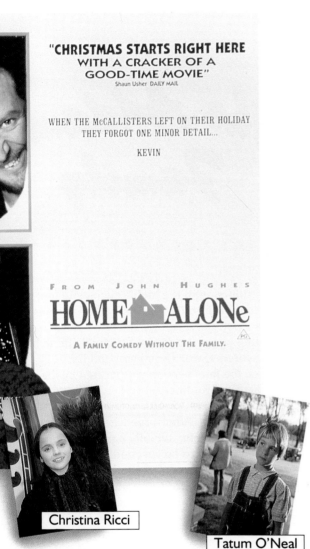

"CHRISTMAS STARTS RIGHT HERE
WITH A CRACKER OF A
GOOD-TIME MOVIE"
Shaun Usher DAILY MAIL

WHEN THE McCALLISTERS LEFT ON THEIR HOLIDAY
THEY FORGOT ONE MINOR DETAIL...

KEVIN

FROM JOHN HUGHES

HOME ALONe

A FAMILY COMEDY WITHOUT THE FAMILY.

Christina Ricci

Tatum O'Neal

E

Put these words in the correct order to make sentences.

1 Shirley Temple's family / her money / if / had saved / a lot richer / would have been / Shirley
2 the best jokes in *The Addams Family* / if / Christina Ricci / she / hadn't had / so successful / wouldn't have been
3 hadn't starred / if / Macaulay Culkin / in *My Girl* / a success / the film / wouldn't have been

F

Write three sentences about your own past life and how it could have been different.

Example: If I had gone to the USA when I was young, I would have learned English a long time ago.

Pronunciation

G 🔲

Listen and say how many words there are in each sentence. Contractions count as two words.

Example: If I'd studied for the exams, I would've passed. = 11 words.

Listen again and repeat the sentences.

H 🗪

In groups, discuss what you would have done in the situations below.

Example: A: What would you have done in situation 1?
B: I'd have gone to Hollywood!

1 A film director chose Daniel's photo and asked him to go to Hollywood to be the star of her next film. Daniel didn't accept.
2 Sandra won a competition for young film directors. She was given money to make a film. She made one about animals.
3 Last summer, David won a competition winning a free holiday. He went on a trip to the Amazon.

Cinema project

I

Find out these key facts about a film star. Then make a fact-file and include a photo.

- date of birth
- hobbies
- family
- first job
- ambitions

24 Producing films

A

Match these descriptions with five of the jobs in the diagram.

Example: 1 = art director

1 The person who supervises the costumes and designs the set.
2 The person in charge of photography.
3 The people who provide the money to produce the film.
4 The person who writes the script.
5 The person who directs the filming.

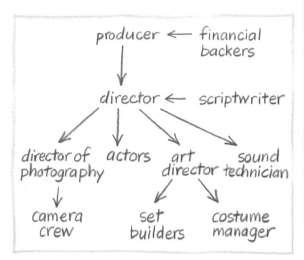

The production of the highly successful film *The Addams Family* was marked by a series of crises. First, the script for the film had to be rewritten again and again. Originally done by
5 scriptwriters Carol Thompson and Larry Wilson, the final version was written by the novelist Paul Rudnick.

Then the twenty weeks of filming were full of minor disasters. After three weeks the director,
10 Barry Sonnenfield, actually passed out on set and filming had to be suspended until he recovered. Not long after that, the director of photography, Owen Roizman, walked out, to go to another movie. Then, his replacement,
15 Gayl Tattersoll, was rushed off to hospital for several days. Next came the actors, with leading actor Raul Julia (Gomez) off with eye problems and Christopher Lloyd (Uncle Fester) nearly losing his ear in a fight scene!
20 Worse than all this, however, were the financial problems for producer Scott Rudin. Three-quarters of the way through the film the backers of the movie, Orion Pictures, decided to sell the film to Paramount Pictures because
25 of desperate money problems.

Sonnenfield and Rudin had a tough time but they managed to concentrate on the shooting of the film. 'I always try to remember two things,' said the sensible Rudin on set. 'One,
30 how good the movie is. And two . . . that it's almost over!'

B

In pairs, list the things which might go wrong during the production of a film. Then read the text and find out what went wrong during the production of *The Addams Family*.

Example: An actor may become ill.

C

Which of the jobs from the diagram in exercise A are mentioned in the text? Who are doing the jobs?

Example: scriptwriters = Carol Thompson, Larry Wilson and Paul Rudnick

Language focus:

REPORTED REQUESTS / ORDERS

D

Listen to a director in three situations. Are the sentences in the table true or false?

. . . . .	. . . . .	. . . . .	. . . . .
1 The director	asked	the art director	to change the colour of the table.
2 The director	told	the actress	to repeat the scene.
3 The producer	asked	the director	not to spend a lot of money.

Copy the table and put these words at the top of the correct column.

- ask/tell ● subject ● action ● object

E

Put these words and expressions in the correct order to make sentences.

1 asked / to give him more money / the financial backers / the producer
2 the actress / to shout more loudly / told / the director
3 to make an artificial street / told / the art director / the set builders

F

Read what the people below say to each other and guess what jobs they do.

Example:
Pat to Jeremy: 'Can you change that hat, please?'
Pat = art director
Jeremy = costume manager

1 Tarquin to Damian: 'Can you look out of the window and smile?'
2 Camilla to Daniel: 'Bring the camera over here.'
3 Stephanie to Anna: 'Can you finish filming next week?'
4 Rob to Emilio: 'Rewrite this part of the film.'

Then report the requests and orders.

Example:
Pat asked Jeremy to change the hat.

G

In pairs, imagine you are in a film studio and it is very noisy. Take turns to be the director giving instructions to an actor/actress.

Example:
A: Now, walk towards the door.
B: Sorry?
A: I told you to walk towards the door!

25 Making your own films

A

Look at the students making their own film. What jobs are they doing? What equipment are they using?

B 📼

Listen to two scenes from the film. Answer these questions.

1 Why does the girl want to go to London?
2 What is her mother's reaction?
3 What is her father's reaction?
4 What is her teacher's reaction?

Pronunciation

C 📼

Listen to six sentences from the scenes. How do the speakers sound? Choose from these words.

sad / sleepy / worried / angry / happy / relaxed / nervous / polite

Example: 1 = relaxed

Listen again and repeat the sentences.

Function focus:

ASKING FOR, GIVING AND REFUSING PERMISSION

D 📼

Listen again to the scenes in exercise B. Match the questions with the replies.

1 Is it all right if I go to London next month?
2 Can I go to the cinema tomorrow night?
3 Could I have a word with you?
4 Would it be all right if I took the day off school?

a) No, certainly not.
b) Yes, of course.
c) I'm afraid you can't.
d) OK, yes you can.

Grade the replies. Copy and complete the table.

Giving permission		Refusing permission	
++	+	–	– –
Yes, of course.			

E 💬

In pairs, act out the following situations. When you act, think about your tone of voice (angry, sad, happy, etc.).

1 A: You are a teenager. Ask your mother/father if you can have a motorbike.
  B: You are the mother or father.
2 A: You are a teacher.
  B: You ask your teacher if you can leave school early to play in a basketball match.
3 A: You are staying with your aunt and uncle. Ask if you can phone a friend in Australia.
  B: You are the aunt or uncle.
4 A: You are a teenager. You have planned to go out with your friends on Saturday night.
  B: You are the mother or father. You want your son/daughter to babysit on Saturday night while you go to the cinema.

Cinema project

F ✎

In groups, write down some ideas for your own film and save them for Lesson 27. Think of these things:

● kind of film: romance/cowboy/suspense
● main character(s)
● other characters
● situation at the start
● storyline – what happens
● number of scenes in the film (maximum 3 or 4)

Who said that?

When Humphrey Bogart was introduced to Rock Hudson at a party, he said, 'Rock – huh?' 'Yes, sir,' Hudson replied. 'Well,' said Bogart, 'You look pretty soft to me, Rock.'

26 Animal wrangler

A

In pairs, discuss these questions.

1 What animals have you seen 'acting' in films?
2 Which animals do you think are easiest to train?
3 Do you think it is cruel to use animals in films?

B

Read the text and choose the best answer, a, b or c.

1 Clint Rowe trains:
   a) fish.   b) wolves.   c) dogs.
2 They had a problem on the coast because there was no:
   a) rain.   b) snow.   c) mashed potato.
3 The dog, Jed, will do what you want if he feels:
   a) patient.   b) tired.   c) secure.
4 Rowe believes it's important to have a rest:
   a) when the dogs are tired.
   b) when the dogs have done some tricks.
   c) when the director is tired.
5 According to Rowe, how many film crews are a problem?
   a) 90%   b) 50%   c) 10%

Who said that?

'Some of my best leading men have been horses and dogs!'
(Elizabeth Taylor, actress)

CLINT ROWE

Clint Rowe is the top animal wrangler, a wrangler being someone who trains animals for the movies. He trains dogs and has just got back from
5 Alaska, where he has been with Jed, a 15-year-old half-wolf, half-dog who stars in the film *White Fang*.

'We were up on the coast and the rain came and washed away the
10 snow! Eventually we used potato flakes to simulate the snow.'
However, the film crew's problems weren't over.

'Unfortunately,' Rowe remembers
15 with a smile, 'when the flakes got wet they turned into mashed potato, and the animals started eating it!'

To train animals takes time and patience.
20 'In *White Fang* we had to persuade Jed to put his head underwater to catch a fish, which he didn't want to do. Jed doesn't like water, you see. We took it very slowly and eventually
25 he did it. Usually if the dog feels secure, he'll do whatever you want.'

Isn't it cruel to use animals like this? Rowe doesn't think so.

'They enjoy doing tricks.'
30 But he thinks it is important for directors to stop when the dogs are tired.

'I'm using a special trailer on this trip, so that the dogs have somewhere
35 to relax when they're not working. I've been on jobs with problems about rest periods, but 90 per cent of film crews are fine. The 10 per cent that aren't, I really believe should be
40 punished.'

Language focus:

REPEATED STATEMENTS

REPORTED STATEMENTS

C

Look at the reported statements in the box. Find the actual words that Clint said in the text. The first two are done for you.

> 1 He told the interviewer that rain had washed away the snow.
>   *'Rain washed away the snow.'*
> 2 He said Jed doesn't like water.
>   *'Jed doesn't like water.'*
> 3 He said if the dog felt secure he would do whatever you wanted.
> 4 He told the interviewer animals enjoy doing tricks.
> 5 He said he was using a special trailer on that trip.
> 6 He said he had been on jobs with problems.

(Notice that when we report people saying things which are still true at the time we report them, we *sometimes* don't change the verb tense.)

Find two sentences in the box where the verb tense doesn't change.

D

When we report what someone said, we usually make changes in the verb tense. Copy and complete the table.

Direct speech	Reported speech
present simple	. . . . .
present continuous	past continuous
past simple	. . . . .
present perfect	. . . . .
will	*would*

Find examples of the changes in the sentences in exercise C.

Example: 1 washed → had washed = past simple → past perfect

E

Imagine you have just done the interview below. Write a report of it. Be careful to make only *necessary* changes to verb tenses.

'My name's Jill White and I work with horses in films. I've worked in lots of westerns and some historical films. At the moment I am working on a film about Genghis Khan. The Mongols were really fantastic riders. Soon I am going to Russia where we are going to start filming. I think it'll be great fun!'

Example: Her name is Jill White and she told me . . .

F

In pairs, ask and answer five questions about films. Then report the interview to a different partner.

Example: A: When did you go to the cinema for the first time?
            B: I went to the cinema for the first time when I was three.

59

27 Fluency

A LEARN TO LEARN

Which of these suggestions can help you when you watch films or television in English?

1 Before you start watching, try to guess what it will be about.
2 If you know what it will be about, write down a list of words that you think may be in the film or programme.
3 While you are watching, try to follow the story through the pictures.
4 Stop watching if you don't understand everything.
5 Remember that to watch a film you only need to understand a little of the dialogue.
6 If you are watching something on video, use the pause and rewind buttons.
7 When it has finished, grade it for difficulty (10 = very, very difficult).
8 Think about the characters which were the easiest to understand and why (how fast they spoke, accents, etc.).

B LEARN TO LEARN

Look at the cover of the video. What do you think it will be about? In pairs, make a list of ten words you think will be in the story.

C

Listen to the summary of *The Emerald Forest* and put the sentences below in the correct order.

Example:
1 Bill goes to build a dam in the Amazon.

● After ten years, Bill finds Tommy.
● He shows his wife and children where he works.
● Tommy grows up with the Indians.
● The dam is destroyed and Tommy returns to the forest.
● Bill goes to build a dam in the Amazon.
● His son, Tommy, is stolen by some Indians.
● Tommy asks his father to help the Indians to destroy the dam.

D LEARN TO LEARN

Look at the Module check on page 107 and grade the listening in exercise C for difficulty.

E

In pairs, interview your partner about a film star. Write down the information. Then guess who the star is. Student A looks at number 3 on page 108. Student B looks at number 3 on page 110.

F

Write a report of the interview you did in exercise E.

Stage 1 Use your notes to plan two paragraphs:
      1 personal information
      2 cinema career
Stage 2 Use your plans to write the report.
Stage 3 Give your report to another student to evaluate
        out of ten.

Cinema project

G

**You are going to perform your own film. Form groups. Each
group chooses a director.**

Stage 1 Read out your ideas for films from the project in
        Lesson 25. Choose one.
Stage 2 Everybody helps to write the script.
Stage 3 The director chooses an actor for each part and
        organises any equipment you have (cassette player,
        lights, video camera).
Stage 4 Do some 'rehearsals' for the film.
Stage 5 Perform it in front of the rest of the class and, if
        possible, video it.

H

**In groups, collect all the written material you have for your
project. Organise it as a magazine or poster and display it
in the classroom.**

> **Did you know?**
>
> Mickey Mouse, the famous
> cartoon character, was first
> called Mortimer Mouse.

28 Revision

Language practice

A

Grammar game. In two teams, take turns to say a sentence using 'direct speech'. The other team has to change it to 'reported speech'. The teacher decides if it is correct and you get a point if it is. The first team to get ten points wins.

Example: A: Miguel has been to London twice.
B: She said that Miguel had been to London twice.

B

In the same teams, take turns to speculate about the picture story below, using the third conditional. If your sentence is correct, your team gets a point.

Example: If he had woken up on time, he wouldn't have missed the train.

Learner training

C

Listen to an interview with a student. He makes eight mistakes. Grade them like this:

★★★★★ = a horrible mistake, impossible to understand
★★★ = a bad mistake at this level
★ = not very bad

Now listen again and correct his mistakes.

Vocabulary

D

Which of these words are similar in your language? Is the meaning the same or different?

magnificent (excellent/ fantastic) /
sensible (reasonable) /
an adventure (exciting activity/experience) /
exciting (causing strong feelings / not calm) /
to concentrate (to direct attention to) /
actually (really/in fact) /
terrible (very bad)

Look through the module and find five more words that are similar in your language. Check that the meaning is the same.

Pronunciation

E 📼

Listen to these four vowel sounds.

Group 1	Group 2	Group 3	Group 4
/ɔ:/ orphan	/ɒ/ often	/ɑ:/ after	/ʌ/ other

Listen to the pairs of words and put them into the correct group according to the sounds.

Example: 1 = Group 1 and Group 4

Look through the module and find two more words with each of the sounds. Use the mini-dictionary to help you.

Test yourself

F 📼

Listen to the situations and guess where the people are. Then listen again and report what the people said.

Example: 1 in a classroom

He asked Helen to close the window.

G

Complete these sentences.

1 If I'd had enough money, I . . . . . bought those jeans.
2 She . . . . . done better in the writing task if she . . . . . brought her dictionary to class.
3 The film . . . . . been more exciting if the actors . . . . . been better.
4 If he . . . . . spoken English all the time in class, he . . . . . passed that exam.
5 The actor . . . . . walked out if the director . . . . . told him to do it again.

H
Do the Module check on page 107.

Do the Module check on page 107.

Language check

THE THIRD CONDITIONAL

If he **hadn't made** *Home Alone*, he **wouldn't have met** the President of the United States.
What **would have happened** if he **had made** more films?
If Shirley's family **had saved** her money, she **would have been** a lot richer.

REPORTED REQUESTS / ORDERS

The director **told** the actress **to repeat** the scene.
The director **asked** her **to change** the table.
The producer **asked** the director **not to spend** more money.
She **told** him **not to stand** next to the window.

REPORTED STATEMENTS

He **told** the interviewer that he **had been** up on the coast.
He **said** animals **enjoy doing** tricks.
He **said** that his next film **would be** a success.
He **told** the interviewer that Jed **doesn't like** water.

---

29 Inventions and discoveries

A

electric light bulb

B

discovery of radium

C

silicon chip showing integrated circuit

D

petrol-driven car

E

early steam engine

A

Match the pictures with these people and dates.

Hero of Alexandria in AD 100 / Thomas Edison in 1879 /
Karl Benz in 1885 / Marie Curie in 1911 / Lise Meitner
in 1939 / Texas Instruments in 1958

B 📼

**Science quiz. In groups, listen to the descriptions of
different inventions and discoveries. The first group to
guess what is being described wins. You only have one
guess!**

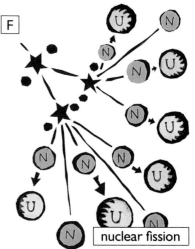

F

nuclear fission

Language focus: PASSIVES

C

Listen again to the first description in the quiz and complete the sentences in the box.

> 1 This instrument . . . . . be considered the most important in the history of communication.
> 2 New technology . . . . . developed.
> 3 Before satellites existed, connections . . . . . made by cables.
> 4 The first long-distance connection . . . . . set up in 1884.
> 5 This instrument . . . . . thought of by Alexander Bell.
> 6 They . . . . . used in private homes and public places.

D

Match the sentences in exercise C with these tenses.

- present simple passive (*is/are done*)
- past simple passive (*was/were done*)
- present perfect passive (*have/has been done*)
- passive with modal verb (*can/could/might/ must be done*)

Why do sentences 3 and 5 contain expressions with *by*. Why don't the others?

Did you know?

The modern toilet (the water closet) was invented by J. Harington in 1589.

E

Write sentences about the inventions and discoveries in exercise A. Use these cues.

1 the telephone / invent
2 the electric lightbulb / invent
3 a steam engine / design
4 silicon chips / produce
5 radium / discover
6 a petrol-driven car / build
7 the first article on nuclear fission / publish

Example: The telephone was invented by Alexander Bell in 1876.

F

In pairs, test your partner on the history of science and scientists. Student A looks at number 4 on page 108. Student B looks at number 4 on page 110.

Pronunciation: SENTENCE STRESS

G

Listen to five sentences and say how many words are in each sentence. Dates count as one word.

Example: 1 The first television programme was made by the BBC in 1936.
= 11

H

Listen again to the sentences in exercise G. Are the words *was* and *were* usually stressed or unstressed? Practise saying the sentences quickly to your partner.

30 Science friction

A
Say how many science lessons you have at school every week. Which of the subjects below do you study?

● physics ● chemistry ● biology

B
Read the experiment about making a hovercraft. Which of the scientific principles below does it illustrate?

● the law of gravity ● electricity ● the force of friction

C
Read the experiment again and put the pictures in the correct order.

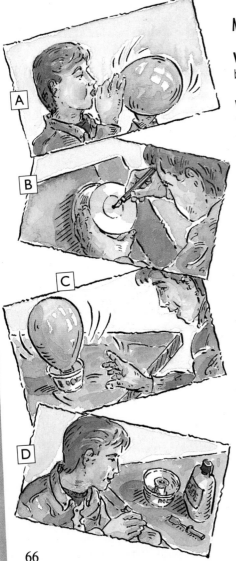

MAKE A HOVERCRAFT

What you need
balloon / margarine tub with a flat bottom / cotton reel / glue

What to do with it
Make a small hole in the centre of the margarine tub *to* let air pass through. Then, glue the cotton reel inside the tub *so that* the middle of it goes over the hole. Let it dry well *otherwise* the cotton reel comes off. Now try to flick the tub across a smooth table *with* your finger. It doesn't go very far, does it? How can we make it go further? Easy! *By using* a balloon. Blow up the balloon and put the end over the cotton reel. Cover the hole in the bottom of the tub with your finger *so that* the air does not come out. Then take your finger away *so* the air starts to come out of the hole and lifts the tub off the table. *Just by* flicking it across a smooth table, you can make it go really fast!

How does it work?
When you flick the tub across the table without the help of the balloon, it stops. Friction between the tub and the table slows it down. But when you use the balloon, it blows out air underneath the tub. Now, there is only friction between the air and the tub. This friction is really small, so when you flick the tub this time it moves easily. A hovercraft works just like the tub: it blows air underneath it – not from a balloon but from a big engine.

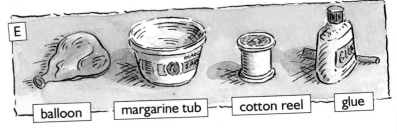

balloon — margarine tub — cotton reel — glue

Function focus: GIVING INSTRUCTIONS

D

Look at the examples in the box.

Why do we make a hole in the tub?	→ *To* let air pass through.
How can we make it go further?	→ *By using* a balloon.

Read the text again. Note which words in *italics* explain *why* we do something and those which explain *how* to do it.

E

Look at the example in the box. Notice that the imperative is used for giving instructions. Then find more examples of the imperative in the text.

> *Make a small hole . . .*

F

Look at the pictures and write the instructions for making a rocket.

Stage 1 Match the verbs below with the pictures. You can use the mini-dictionary.
blow up / stick / let go / tie / thread

Stage 2 Plan the instructions in three parts:
1 what you need   2 how to do it   3 how it works

Stage 3 Use the verbs to write the instructions. Explain why and how to do things.

Stage 4 Give the instructions to your partner to check.

G

Bet you can't . . .! In pairs, give and receive instructions and try to follow them. If you don't understand, ask your partner to explain. Student A looks at number 5 on page 109, Student B looks at number 5 on page 111.

Examples:
B: Sorry, how do you do that?
A: With a pair of scissors.
B: Why do I have to do that?
A: To try to make it smaller.

Find out why it was impossible to do it.

Example:
B: Why couldn't I . . .?
A: Because . . .

Did you know?

Cars take much longer to slow down and stop when it is raining. This is because the water on the road reduces the friction between the car and the surface of the road.

31 Understanding computers

A

In groups, list the places where computers are used and report your list to the class.

Example: in banks

B

Match the objects on the desk with these words.

printer / VDU / disk / keyboard

C

Read the description of how a computer works. Then complete the diagram.

```
┌─────────────────────────┐
│         INPUT           │
│  1 . . . . . or 2 . . . . . │
└─────────────────────────┘
            ↓
┌─────────────────────────────────────────┐
│  Central Processing Unit → ┌──────────────┐ │
│                            │ ROM (memory) │ │
│                            └──────────────┘ │
│                                   ↓          │
│                            ┌──────────────┐ │
│                            │ 3 . . . . . (memory) │ │
│                            └──────────────┘ │
└─────────────────────────────────────────┘
            ↓
┌─────────────────────────┐
│  4 . . . . . or 5 . . . . . │
│         OUTPUT          │
└─────────────────────────┘
            ↓
┌─────────────────────────┐
│      6 . . . . .        │
│    (telephone line)     │
└─────────────────────────┘
            ↓
     another computer
```

UNDERSTANDING COMPUTERS

----·--·--·--·--·--·--·----

Today we use many machines, but often we don't know how they work. For example, we drive cars but maybe know nothing about car engines. It's the same with computers. Secretaries use them to write letters, writers use them to write books, bankers use them to store and transfer information; but not many people know how they work.

There are three basic parts of a computer: the input unit, the central processing unit (CPU), and the output unit.

Let's imagine you want to send or store some information using a computer. It may be something you want to keep, like a friend's address, or something you want to print out, like your English homework! First of all, you send the information to the CPU from a keyboard, which is like a typewriter. Alternatively, the information may already be on a disk and can be sent straight to the CPU.

When the information reaches the CPU it is translated into a special code by the CPU's 'brain', the ROM (Read Only Memory). With this, the CPU reads the information and then it is stored in a memory called RAM (Random Access Memory).

Finally, the information is sent to the output unit. It can be displayed on the VDU, which is like a television, or can be printed out using a printer.

The information can also be sent to other computers using a 'modem'. This is a special way of sending electronic signals along telephone lines to other computers anywhere in the world.

D

Read the text again. Find the words and expressions which link the different stages of the process.

Example: First of all, . . .

68

Function focus: EXPLAINING USES

E

Match the objects with the uses.

1	A printer	a)	is for communicating with other computers.
2	A VDU	b)	is for putting data into a computer.
3	A modem	c)	is for displaying data.
4	A keyboard	d)	is for printing out data.

F

Choose some of the objects below and explain what they are used for.

a ruler / pans / a fridge / glue / a rubber / a brush / a blackboard / a schoolbag / a sink / shelves

Examples: A ruler is for measuring things.
Pans are for cooking things.

G

Guessing game. In groups, Student A thinks of a machine or tool. The others must guess what it is, asking only ten questions.

Example: B: Is it large?
A: No.
C: Do you use it for travelling?
A: No.
D: Do you use it for cleaning things?
A: No.
B: Do you use it for studying?
A: Yes.
C: Can you use it for writing?
A: No.
D: Can you use it for doing calculations?
A: Yes.
B: Is it a . . . ?

H

Look at the pictures and stages in the process of making silicon chips. Describe the process by linking the stages and using the passive.

Example: First of all, silicon is made into crystals from sand.

Stage 1 Silicon made into crystals from sand

Stage 2 Crystal shaped into long rods
Stage 3 Rods cut into thin slices

Stage 4 Circuit designed on computer
Stage 5 Design placed on silicon slices by photographic process
Stage 6 Circuits treated with chemicals

Stage 7 Slices cut up into individual chips

32 Science and you

A

In groups, talk about the differences you can find between the two pictures.

Examples: A: In picture A the girl's got a leather bag.
B: In picture B the bag's made of plastic.
C: In picture B there's a fridge.
D: In picture A there isn't a fridge.

B

Listen to the girl in picture B talking to her grandmother. List five differences between their lives.

Example: 1 The girl does her homework with a calculator. Her grandmother had to do mental arithmetic.

Language focus:

USED TO / TO BE USED TO

C

Listen again and complete these sentences.

1	GRANDMOTHER:	We used to . . . . . all those mathematical calculations in our heads. We didn't use to . . . . . calculators and computers.
2	GIRL:	I'm used to . . . . . with my computer now, but it was difficult at first.
3	GRANDMOTHER:	I'm not used to . . . . . I did it once and it was terrible.
4	GIRL:	When I was little I was afraid of flying, but now I'm used to . . . . .

D

Copy and complete the box for the two different structures using these words.

-ing words / infinitive / noun or pronoun

> *be used to* + ¹ . . . . . or ² . . . . .
> *used to* + ³ . . . . .

Which structure describes:

a) something that happened regularly in the past, but does not happen now?
b) something that is easy or familiar?

E

Write sentences about three objects in the pictures.

Example: People didn't use to have calculators, but now we're used to them.

F ✎

In pairs, prepare three questions to ask what another pair used to do when they were six years old. In groups of four, take turns to ask and answer the questions.

Example: A: When you were six, when did you use to go to bed?
B: I used to go to bed at seven o'clock.
C: I used to go to bed at eight. Now I go at eleven.

G ✎

In pairs, take turns to be a reporter and interview someone. Student A looks at number 6 on page 109. Student B looks at number 6 on page 111.

Example: A: Are you used to living in a big house?
B: No, I'm not. My parents used to have a small house.

33 Lost contributions

A 🗪

In groups, talk about these things.

- How many famous scientists can you name?
- Are boys better at science than girls?

B

Read the text and match these titles with the paragraphs.

- Women Scientists in History
- The Discovery of DNA
- No Famous Names
- Problems for Women Scientists

WOMEN IN SCIENCE

[1] Can you name five famous scientists? You probably can: Einstein, Newton, Leonardo da Vinci, Galileo, Edison . . . The list goes on. But how many women
5 scientists can you name? Madame Curie and, er . . . The list seems to stop before *it* starts. Why is this? Is it because there aren't any women scientists? Is it because women aren't as
10 clever as men? Or because women aren't interested in science? The answer to all of these questions is 'no'.

[2] There have been women scientists since earliest times in history. Women
15 took care of the sick and made medicines from plants. *They* invented early farming machines and machines to make clothes and pots. We know that in Ancient Egypt women were
20 active in astronomy, medicine and chemistry. There were women scientists in Ancient Greece, too, but we know little about *them*.

[3] In more recent times, women have
25 become involved in science in a big way, but there are reasons why so few are household names. *Many* designed things, but didn't have enough money to see their inventions become a
30 reality; others had ideas, but were not allowed to go to university, so asked men to convert their ideas into actual constructions; and some women's ideas have been 'borrowed' by men.

[4] 35 The work of Rosalind Franklin is a good example. In 1951 she began analysing the structure of DNA,
40 the substance which carries the body's genetic code. A year later, unknown to *her*, a copy of one of her papers and her best photograph of a form
45 of DNA were shown to two men scientists, Watson and Crick. *They* were working in the same area. The photograph was extremely important. Rosalind began working on another
50 project, and in 1958 she died. In 1962, Watson and Crick were given the Nobel Prize for their work on DNA, and today are believed to be the discoverers of its structure. But who
55 first photographed the structure of DNA? Rosalind *Who*?

C

Read the text again. What do the words, which are in *italics* in the text, refer to?

Example: it (line 7) = the list

it (line 7) / They (line 16) / them (line 23) / Many (line 27) / her (line 43) / They (line 46)

Language focus:

ARTICLES: THE, A, AN

D

Look at the rules and examples in the box. Then read the text again and find more examples of these rules.

> You use *the*:
> 1 when you are talking about something specific.
>   *Example:* **The list** goes on. (line 4)
>
> 2 when you refer to something you have mentioned before.
>   *Example:* . . . her best photograph (was) shown to two men scientists. **The photograph** was extremely important. (line 48)
>
> You use *a* or *an*:
> 1 when you mention something for the first time.
>   *Example:* **a copy** . . . was shown. (line 43)
>
> 2 when you refer to someone or something without giving details.
>   *Example:* I gave her **a book**.
>
> You don't use *the* or *a*:
> 1 when you talk about people or things in general.
>   *Example:* . . . **women** aren't interested in **science**. (lines 10 and 11)
>
> 2 when you refer to countries or some places you go to often.
>   *Examples:* He lives in **Italy**.
>   She goes to **school** every day.

E

Read about three more women scientists and fill in the gaps with articles *when necessary*.

Example: 1 = a

Kathleen Kenyon (1906–1978) was ¹ . . . . . great archaeologist. She studied ² . . . . . human history. From 1952 to 1958 she worked near ³ . . . . . ancient city of Jericho in ⁴ . . . . . Jordan. She was able to date ⁵ . . . . . city back to 7000 BC, making Jericho ⁶ . . . . . oldest city in ⁷ . . . . . world. This showed ⁸ . . . . . importance of ⁹ . . . . . cities in ¹⁰ . . . . . development of ¹¹ . . . . . civilisation.

Kathleen Lonsdale (1903–71) was ¹² . . . . . brilliant research scientist. At ¹³ . . . . . school, she had to take lessons at ¹⁴ . . . . . boys' school because girls couldn't do ¹⁵ . . . . . science at her school. She developed ¹⁶ . . . . . X-ray method to measure ¹⁷ . . . . . distance between diamond atoms, and applied her work to ¹⁸ . . . . . medical problems.

Margaret Burbidge is ¹⁹ . . . . . astronomer. She was ²⁰ . . . . . first woman director of ²¹ . . . . . Royal Greenwich Observatory.

Pronunciation

F 📼

Listen to the two ways of pronouncing 'th'.

Group 1	Group 2
/ð/ *the*	/θ/ *thing*

Listen and put these words into the correct group.

think / thin / this / thick / these / there / they / through / their / three / other

Now practise saying the words with a partner.

34 Fluency

A 📼

Listen to the description of Lise Meitner's life and work. Are the statements below true or false?

Lise Meitner

1 Lise Meitner was born in Australia.
2 She was a professor of physics in Germany.
3 She discovered a new radioactive substance in 1917.
4 She had to run away in 1938.
5 She went to Switzerland.
6 She proposed the idea of nuclear fission in 1935.

B 📼

Science quiz. How much have you learnt from this module? Listen and write down the answers to the questions.

Example: 1 Alexander Bell

C ✍

In pairs, take turns to describe a diagram for your partner to draw. Student A looks at number 7 on page 109. Student B looks at number 7 on page 111.

D ✍

Science survey. In groups, ask each other the questions below. Write down the answers. Keep the results for exercise E.

1 Do you like science lessons?
2 Which is your favourite scientific subject – biology, chemistry or physics?
3 Are you good at mathematics?
4 Would you like to do more science experiments in school?
5 Have you ever used a computer?
6 Have you ever bought a science book or magazine?

E 📖 LEARN TO LEARN

Look at the diagrams and say which of these things they are used for.

● writing down ideas
● classifying vocabulary
● showing information
● explaining how things work

Now draw a bar graph to show the results of the survey you did in exercise D.

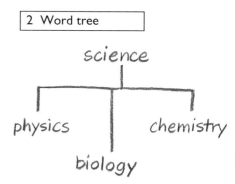

74

3 Pie chart

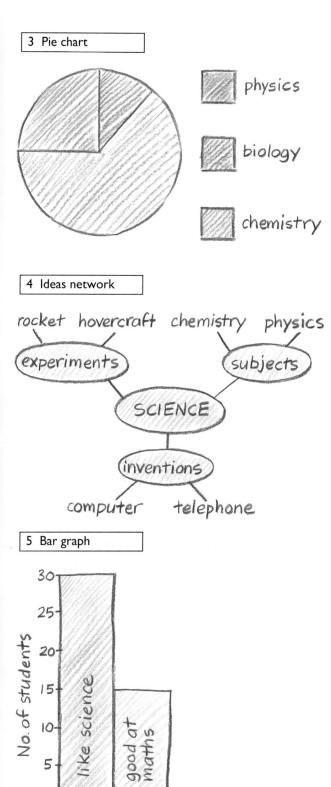

physics

biology

chemistry

4 Ideas network

rocket hovercraft chemistry physics

experiments subjects

SCIENCE

inventions

computer telephone

5 Bar graph

No. of students (vertical axis: 30, 25, 20, 15, 10, 5)

like science

good at maths

F ✎

Look at the diagram and use the notes to explain how a periscope works. Use these expressions in the correct order to link your sentences.

First of all / After that / Finally / Next / Then

Example: First of all, light from an object enters the periscope.

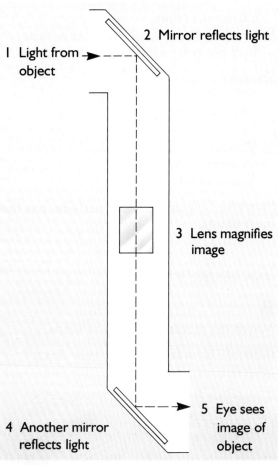

1 Light from object

2 Mirror reflects light

3 Lens magnifies image

4 Another mirror reflects light

5 Eye sees image of object

G LEARN TO LEARN

Give your explanation of how a periscope works to your partner. Your partner grades it 1–3, like this:

3 = very clear and easy to understand
2 = quite clear
1 = difficult to understand, confusing

35 Revision

Language practice

A
Divide into two teams.

Team A Think of a sentence in the active.
Team B Change the sentence into the passive.

Score, like this:
For each correct passive sentence you get one point.
If a sentence is impossible to change then there is a point for the other team.

Example:
A: Bell invented the telephone in 1876.
B: The telephone is invented for Bell in 1876.
T: Wrong! One point to A. The correct answer is: The telephone *was* invented *by* Bell in 1876.

Stop after five minutes and see who has the most points.

Vocabulary

B
Match the pictures with these verbs.

think of / blow up / turn on / slow down / print out

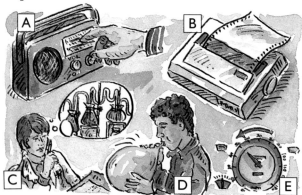

Now write a sentence using each verb.

Example: She printed out her homework.

Pronunciation

C
Listen and look at these word stress patterns.

Pattern 1	*Pattern 2*	*Pattern 3*
☐ ☐ ☐	☐ ☐☐	☐☐☐ ☐
instrument	direction	biology

Listen and put these words into groups according to their stress patterns.

technology / telephone / reaction / invention / atomic / astrology / electric / instruction / photograph / geology / computer / periscope

Now practise saying the words with a partner.

Learner training

D 🔲 LEARN TO LEARN
In dictionaries, stress is marked on the phonetic transcription of words, like this:

technology / tek'nɒlədʒi /
telephone / 'telɪfəʊn /
reaction / ri'ækʃən /

Look through your vocabulary book and mark the stress on the important words, like this:

☐	☐	☐
technology	telephone	reaction

Then check the stress in the mini-dictionary.

Test yourself

E

Read the text and fill in the gaps with the correct form of the words below *when necessary.*

to be / the / a / an

¹. . . . . first calculating machine, called the abacus, ². . . . . used by the Babylonians in about 3000 BC. In 1834 Charles Babbage designed ³. . . . . machine for calculating, but it was too complicated to build. ⁴. . . . . first real computer ⁵. . . . . made in 1948. Ten years later, Texas Instruments produced ⁶. . . . . chip made of ⁷. . . . . silicon, with ⁸. . . . . integrated circuit. In 1969 ⁹. . . . . American scientist invented ¹⁰. . . . . micro-processor, with ¹¹. . . . . different parts of ¹². . . . . computer on one silicon chip. Now these micro-processors ¹³. . . . . used everywhere: in watches and washing machines, in cars and aeroplanes, and in factories and offices. ¹⁴. . . . . lesson you are doing at this moment ¹⁵. . . . . written using one of them!

F

Correct these sentences.

1 I am use to getting my own breakfast; I do it every day.
2 When she was young she used to going to bed early.
3 I've only been on an aeroplane once; I'm not use to fly.
4 I don't like getting up early, but I used to it.
5 In the 1940s they didn't used to watch much television.

G

Do the Module check on page 107.

Language check

PASSIVES

Micro-processors **are used** in watches and washing machines.
The telephone **was invented** in 1876 by Alexander Bell.
New technology **has been developed**.

USED TO / TO BE USED TO

When I was young we **used to walk** two miles to school.
We **didn't use to do** maths with calculators.
Did you use to have chemistry lessons?
It was difficult at first, but now I **am used to working** with my computer.
English people **aren't used to driving** on the right.

ARTICLES: THE, A, AN

The electric lightbulb was invented by Edison.
A French scientist used **the** first camera. **The** scientist's name was Niépce.
An American scientist invented **the** micro-processor.
Heat is caused by friction.
My brother is at school and my sister goes to university.

A

Read about some different styles of popular music. Use the mini-dictionary to check any difficult words. Match the pictures with the appropriate styles to complete the network.

Example: 1 = gospel

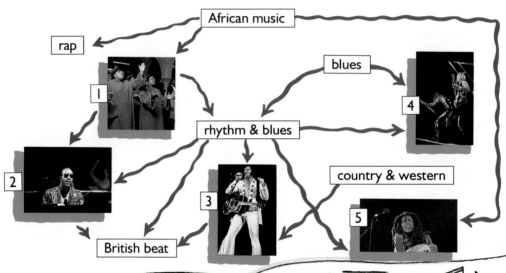

POP STYLES

- **The Blues**: traditional black American music. 'Blue' means 'sad', and many blues songs are about how hard life is.
- **Gospel**: originally sung by African slaves. The happy, emotional songs are still heard in churches in the southern USA.
- **Rhythm and Blues**: black workers in the USA moved from farms to the cities. They mixed the blues with gospel and played it with electric guitars – this became 'rhythm and blues'.
- **Country and Western**: the music of poor white Americans in the 1930s and 1940s. It is still the most popular music in the southern USA.
- **Rock and Roll**: white teenagers in the 1950s discovered rhythm and blues, but many radio stations would not play 'black' music. Elvis Presley was one of the first singers to mix rhythm and blues and country and western. The result was 'rock and roll'.

- **Soul**: a mixture of gospel and rhythm and blues. Some styles are named after the record label (e.g. 'Motown') or they may be given other names such as 'funk' or 'disco'. The most successful 'soul' artists are probably Stevie Wonder and Michael Jackson.
- **British Beat**: the Beatles in the 1960s mixed rhythm and blues, rock and roll, and soul music. The new style was 'beat' music. Groups used drums, bass and two guitars with vocal lead and harmony.
- **Heavy Metal**: a style based on blues and rhythm and blues, but with the electric instruments amplified so they are very loud.
- **Reggae**: this started in Jamaica and is a mixture of music from African roots and rhythm and blues. Bob Marley made it popular.
- **Rap**: in the 1980s DJs in American clubs began half singing and half talking over instrumental records. This is called 'rap'. West African speech rhythms survive in rap.

B

Read the text again and answer these questions.

1 Where did 'rhythm and blues' start?
2 Who was one of the first 'rock and roll' singers?
3 What styles did The Beatles mix to create British Beat music?
4 Who made 'reggae' popular?
5 When did 'rap' start?

C

In pairs, Student A asks questions about the text. Student B answers the questions with the book closed.

Examples: A: Where did 'gospel' come from?
B: From Africa.
A: When did 'country and western' music start?
B: In the 1930s in the southern USA.

D

Listen to some different styles of music. Try to match them with the styles described in the text.

Function focus:

EXPRESSING LIKES AND DISLIKES

E

Listen to the expressions below. How enthusiastic do the people sound? Copy the table and add the expressions to the appropriate column.

★★★	★	—	✕	✕✕✕
I love it.	I like it.	I don't mind it.	I don't like it.	I can't stand it.

I don't mind it. / I love it. / I don't like it. / I can't stand it. /
I like it. / It's quite nice. / I'm crazy about it. / It's OK. /
It doesn't appeal to me. / It's horrible. / It's all right. /
It's fantastic. / I hate it.

Listen again and check your answers.

F

Listen to the music in exercise D again. Write a sentence about each piece of music.

Examples:
I can't stand heavy metal.
Reggae is OK.

G

In groups, give your opinions about the music.

Example:
A: I love reggae.
B: So do I.
C: I don't, I think it's horrible.

Report to the class the most popular kind of music in your group.

H

Copy and complete the lists with the words below. Use the mini-dictionary to help you.

bass guitar / gospel / harmony /
rap / drums / rhythm / disco /
electric guitar / vocal lead

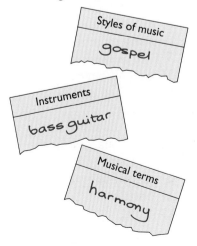

Styles of music
gospel

Instruments
bass guitar

Musical terms
harmony

37 A pop star

A

In pairs, find out your partner's five favourite pop stars.

B

Read the magazine article. Match these titles with the paragraphs.

- Plans for the future
- The interview
- Success
- Starting off

C

True or false?

1 Dwayne said he would like to have a car.
2 Dwayne said he had started off with his brother Reg.
3 The Benefits' music was influenced by Elvis Presley.
4 They have recently made another album.

D

Match the words in *italics* with the best definition.

1 a *glorious* day
  a) dull and cloudy
  b) hot and sunny
  c) rainy
2 We *haven't looked back.*
  a) haven't remembered
  b) have had complete success
  c) have made plans
3 another long, *gruelling* world tour
  a) enjoyable
  b) boring
  c) tiring

80

THE INTERVIEW

This week, Buzz Magazine's reporter Jerry Crowley meets Dwayne Benefit, leader of the successful Benefits rock group.

1 I arrived at Dwayne Benefit's home on a glorious day in August. We'd arranged the interview the night before. I was surprised, as I walked up to his house, not to see a Rolls Royce or swimming pool – the usual trappings of a
5 rich rock star. 'I don't have a car because I don't drive,' he explained later.

2 As we sipped a cool fruit juice, I asked him how it had all started. 'My brother, Reg, and myself used to mess around with instruments in our house. There were always
10 a few friends around and we used to try to write our own songs.' I wondered what their early music was like. 'Well, it was a mixture of styles. My dad had lots of records, Elvis Presley, that sort of thing. We were also influenced by the Beatles, of course.' And so how did these kids
15 become a rock group? 'My brother, Reg, put an advert in the local paper. He said we could play anything. It wasn't true, of course!'

3 Dwayne has come a long way since those early days in London. 'The present line-up came together in 1984 –
20 that's me on bass, Reg on keyboards, Danny on lead guitar and Jackie on drums. We began to develop our own style and people started getting interested in us. We made "The Lost Detail", our first album, in 1987, and began touring in Britain and Europe. Since then we haven't
25 looked back.'

4 The Benefits have been out of the public eye for some time now. Dwayne seems to be enjoying doing nothing in particular. 'Er, I suppose I am quite lazy! But we're going into the studio next year to make another album and then,
30 probably another long, gruelling world tour.' Is it a hard life? 'Not really,' says Dwayne, pouring another drink.

Language focus: REPORTED QUESTIONS

E

Look at the questions in the box. Then read the rules about direct and reported questions below.

Direct question	Reported question
'**Why** don't you have a car?' →	He asked him **why** he didn't have a car.
'**How** did it all start?' →	He asked him **how** it had all started.
'Is it a hard life?' →	He asked him **whether** it was a hard life.
'**What** was your early music like?' →	He asked him **what** their early music had been like.
'Will you tour again?' →	He asked him **if** he would tour again.

1 **Word order**: In reported questions the word order is different from direct questions.
Direct questions: auxiliary / subject / main verb
Reported questions: subject / auxiliary or main verb
2 **Question words**: In reporting questions which do not have a question word (*who/what/how*), you use *if* or *whether*.
3 **Punctuation**: In reported questions there are no question marks (?) and inverted commas (' ').
4 **Tense changes**: The changes of tenses for reported questions are the same as those for reported statements.
Example: past simple to past perfect / *will* to *would*, etc.

F

Look at the questions and report what the interviewer asked Dwayne. Use the table in Lesson 26 to help you with changes of tense.

Example: 1 He asked him if 'Dwayne Benefit' was his real name.

1 Is 'Dwayne Benefit' your real name?
2 What are your musical influences?
3 When did you make your first album?
4 Have you written any new songs recently?
5 When will you make your next album?

Answer the questions if you can from the magazine article.

G

In groups, each student thinks of a question to ask. Student A whispers the question to Student B. Student B says the answer aloud. The others in the group have to guess what the question was and report it.

Example:
A: (*whispers question*)
B: (*answers aloud*) At ten o'clock.
C: He/She asked you what time you had gone to bed last night.
B: No.
D: He/She asked you what time you got up at weekends.
B: Yes!

Music project

H

Invent your own pop group.

Stage 1 Name the group. Make up names for its members. Decide what instruments and what style of music they play.

Stage 2 Write an advert for a music paper, similar to the Benefits' advertisement in the magazine article.

38 Making an album

A

In groups, discuss the questions below.

1 What do you think are best: records, cassettes or compact discs?
2 What is the name of your favourite album? Who is it by?

B

Listen to the Benefits' manager talking about making a record. Then put the pictures in the correct order.

Example: 1 = picture B

Language focus:

GERUNDS AND INFINITIVES

C

Listen again to the Benefits' manager. Then complete these sentences by putting the verb in brackets into the correct form, gerund (*playing*) or infinitive (*to play*).

1 They *regret* (do) . . . . . that, because there's only one chance to record.
2 . . . basic things like which instruments they'*d like* (use) . . . . .
3 Somebody might *suggest* (add) . . . . . drums or piano.
4 It's not too late to *consider* (do) . . . . . it again.
5 You *need* (get) . . . . . it right if you *want* (sell) . . . . . a lot of albums.

D

Some verbs can take a gerund or an infinitive, but the meaning changes. Match the examples with the definitions.

Example: 1a) = (i)

1 a) The group *stops playing* and starts again.
  b) After you've recorded all the songs you *stop to think* about it all.
    (i) to stop an activity
    (ii) to stop for a specific reason
2 a) I told them to *try playing* different versions.
  b) You must *try to get* it right the first time.
    (i) to make an effort
    (ii) to experiment with something
3 a) 'I don't *remember playing* that!'
  b) I told them to *remember to take* everything.
    (i) to remember something for the future
    (ii) to remember the past

E

Choose the correct form of the verb in these sentences.

Example: 1 = playing

1 I stopped *playing* / *to play* my guitar and went out.
2 She tried *finishing* / *to finish* the book.
3 I remember *buying* / *to buy* my first record.
4 I always remember *taking* / *to take* my identity card with me when I go out.

F

Look at the song below and put the verbs in the correct form. Then listen to the song and check your answers.

> **The Lost Detail**
>
> I've considered (take)[1] . . . . . your advice
> Yes, I remember (make)[2] . . . . . big mistakes
> I regret (say)[3] . . . . . what I did
> I want (be)[4] . . . . . true, and not a fake.
> I've taken time to stop (think)[5] . . . . .
> I don't want our ship of love (sink)[6] . . . . .
> I don't want everything (fail)[7] . . . . .
> So I'm looking for the lost detail.
> You say you'd like (start)[8] . . . . . again
> You want (live)[9] . . . . . in the past
> But you don't regret (do)[10] . . . . . a single thing.
> You were the first and I'm the last.
>
> Words and music by *Dwayne & Reg Benefit*

Music project

G

Design an album cover. On the front put the title and name of your group. On the back put the list of song titles.

39 On stage

A

Read about Liz Berry and answer these questions.

1 What is Liz's job?
2 Where did she first help with rock concerts?
3 How did she find her present job?

Liz Berry

ON TOUR

For big groups, going on tour can be an expensive and complicated business, involving a small army of people – the tour manager, ⁵ promoters, accountants, security staff, publicists and the road crew. Liz Berry is one person in that 'small army'.

Liz Berry has worked for Michael Jackson in ¹⁰ Rome. Thanks to her, the singer's concerts were spectacular visually as well as musically, for Liz is a lighting engineer. She is sent to concerts throughout Europe by her company to sort out problems with lighting ¹⁵ equipment.

Liz didn't enjoy school much, although she left with 'A' levels in English, mathematics and biology. She began studying for an English degree at Manchester University, but ²⁰ never finished the course. In her second year she became the sound and lighting technician for rock concerts held in the student union building.

When she found how much she enjoyed ²⁵ the job, she left university despite her parents' anxiety. She went to study electronics in London for a year, and got her job with the lighting company through an advertisement. Liz enjoys the concerts, the ³⁰ travel and the electronics. Soon she will again leave the workshop where she is based to join another road crew as it tours Europe.

'It's not all glamour, and the hours can be ³⁵ terribly long, but the show must go on!'

B

Choose the best ending according to the text, a, b, or c.

1 Michael Jackson's concerts were spectacular because
   a) they had good music.
   b) they had good lighting.
   c) both the music and lighting were good.
2 Liz didn't enjoy school
   a) but liked English, maths and biology.
   b) and left with no qualifications.
   c) but passed exams in English, maths and biology.
3 Liz's parents
   a) wanted her to leave university.
   b) were worried when she left university.
   c) told her to leave university.

C

Which words in the text fit the definitions? Use the mini-dictionary to help you.

1 very exciting and impressive
2 a period of study
3 worry or concern
4 to continue

Function focus:

MAKING INFORMAL ARRANGEMENTS

D

Listen to the dialogue. Complete the table.

Suggestion	Response
Would you like ¹ . . . . . that new group?	→ Yes, great!
Shall we ² . . . . . on Saturday?	→ Mmm, sounds ³ . . . . .
Could you ⁴ . . . . . the tickets?	→ Yes, OK.
How about ⁵ . . . . . Sue to come?	→ Yes, all right.
Let's ⁶ . . . . . at my place.	→ OK.

Pronunciation: INTONATION

E

Listen again to the dialogue. Mark the responses: enthusiastic (✓) or not interested (✕). Then listen again and repeat the responses.

F ✍

Write five suggestions about things to do. In pairs, make your suggestions to your partner. Reply enthusiastically if you'd really like to go. Reply without enthusiasm if you are not interested.

Example: A: Shall we go to the cinema?
           B: Yes. Great!

G 📼

Listen to the first sound in three words.

Group 1	*Group 2*	*Group 3*
/w/ *would*	/k/ *could*	/g/ *good*

Listen to five sentences which start with these words. Which sentences are incorrect?

Now listen to five more sentences and repeat them.

Music project

H ✍

Write a short review (good or bad) of a concert you have been to or seen on video, like this:

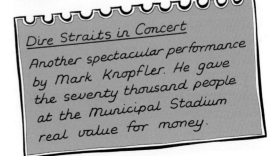

Dire Straits in Concert
Another spectacular performance by Mark Knopfler. He gave the seventy thousand people at the Municipal Stadium real value for money.

40 The violin virtuoso

A 📼

Listen to three pieces of classical music. Choose from the words below to describe how each piece is played.

- slowly and sadly
- fast and spectacularly
- delicately and happily

B

Read the life story of Paganini. Which of the pieces of music that you heard in exercise A do you think he composed?

C

Read the text again and match these titles with the paragraphs.

- Concerts
- Lifestyle
- Childhood appearance
- Starting off
- Teenage success

D

Read the text again and answer these questions.

1 Why did Paganini look very strange as a boy?
2 At what age did he become successful?
3 Why were his concerts spectacular?
4 How was Paganini like a modern pop star?

Niccolò Paganini 1782–1840

1 He was a *very* odd little boy indeed. He was *incredibly* thin and his face was terribly pale. He had burning eyes, hands like bird claws and his long black hair usually hung down *carelessly* on either side of his
5 face.

2 He was *desperately* poor as well. His father was a music teacher and all he had to give his son, Niccolò, was a basic knowledge of music. One day the young Niccolò discovered the violin. He practised hard for
10 hour after hour, day after day, *rarely* stopping to eat or sleep. When he was ten 'Nicco' had his first public concert. He played *brilliantly* and everyone who heard him was completely amazed.

3 From that moment Niccolò Paganini *never* looked
15 back. At the age of fifteen he started to manage everything by himself, booking concert halls, arranging contracts and planning tours. By the time he was sixteen he had composed his famous Caprices, some of the most difficult violin music ever written.

4 20 His concerts were *highly* spectacular. He *always* dressed completely in black, and he looked *really* sinister. *Sometimes* at his concerts he used to act very *strangely*. One of his tricks was to play a very difficult piece, then take out a pair of scissors, cut off three
25 strings and play the same piece of music again on one string only.

5 Paganini became as rich and famous as many modern pop stars. Crowds followed him in the street and even poems were written about him. And he lived
30 very *extravagantly*, becoming a passionate gambler and having love affairs all over Europe. When he died, at the age of fifty-eight, his priceless Guarnerius violin was placed in the City Hall of Genoa, and is known as 'Paganini's widow'. Very *occasionally*, it is taken out
35 and played by some visiting virtuoso.

Language focus: ADVERBS

E

Look at three types of adverbs.

a) **Adverbs of frequency:** describe *how often* something is done.
b) **Adverbs of manner:** describe *how* something is done.
c) **Modifying adverbs:** describe *how good/bad/thin/poor*, etc. someone or something is.

Examples: very (line 1) = c)
carelessly (line 4) = b)
never (line 14) = a)

Now classify these adverbs, which are in *italics* in the text, a, b or c.

incredibly (line 1) / desperately (line 6) / rarely (line 10) / brilliantly (line 12) / highly (line 20) / always (line 20) / really (line 21) / sometimes (line 22) / strangely (line 23) / extravagantly (line 30) / occasionally (line 34)

F

Copy and complete this table. Add to the list of regular adverbs.

	Adjectives	Adverbs
Irregular	good	well
	fast	
	hard	
Regular	brilliant	
	extravagant	
	incredible	

G

Put the adverbs in brackets in the correct place in the sentences.

Example: 1 Mozart played the harpsichord brilliantly from the age of three.

1 Mozart played the harpsichord from the age of three. (brilliantly)
2 From the age of five he could compose music. (very well)
3 By the time he was eight he became popular all over Europe. (incredibly)
4 He had to work as a child. (very hard)
5 He slept in the same bed for more than three nights. (rarely)
6 He wrote some successful operas. (highly)
7 Mozart became a rich man. (never)

H

Listen and decide how the people say this sentence.

'Put your books away.'

Choose from the adverbs below.

politely / angrily / quietly / slowly / loudly / sleepily / nervously / quickly

Example: 1 = slowly

I ✍

In groups, one person says this sentence. The others describe how he/she says it.

'Could you lend me your pen?'

Example: A: Could you lend me your pen?
B: You said it quietly.

41 | Fluency

A

In pairs, find out which of the things below your partner does when he/she listens to pop songs in English.

a) Listens to the songs and tries to understand a few words.
b) Listens to the songs but does not worry about the words.
c) Listens to the songs and tries to write down the words, stopping the cassette and rewinding.
d) Looks at a copy of the words and tries to translate them.

B [LEARN TO LEARN]

Body language. In pairs, discuss your answers to the questionnaire below.

QUESTIONNAIRE

1 What do you do when you meet someone you don't know?
   a) Shake hands with the person.
   b) Kiss the person once or twice.
   c) Hug the person.
   d) Speak but don't touch.
2 Which of the above do you do when you meet a friend in the street?
3 When someone is relaxed and friendly to you, which of these things do they do?

a) Fold their arms and cross their legs.

b) Look at you and smile.

c) Stand quite close to you.

d) Avoid looking at you.

e) Stand a long way from you.

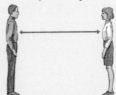

C 📼

Look at the picture. Which of the two people is relaxed and friendly? Which person is nervous?

Guess the answers to these questions.

1 Who suggests going out?
2 What is the reaction of the other person?
3 Do they go out together?

Listen to the dialogue and see if you were right.

D

In pairs, follow the instructions below to act out a similar dialogue to exercise C.

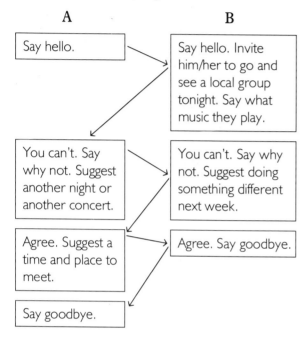

A   B

Say hello. → Say hello. Invite him/her to go and see a local group tonight. Say what music they play.

You can't. Say why not. Suggest another night or another concert. → You can't. Say why not. Suggest doing something different next week.

Agree. Suggest a time and place to meet. → Agree. Say goodbye.

Say goodbye.

Pronunciation

E 📼

Listen and look at the stress of the word *record* in the two sentences below. In which sentence is it a noun and in which is it a verb?

a) The Benefits have just made a new record.

b) They always record their albums in London.

Listen to six sentences using the words below. Mark the stress and write whether the word is a noun or a verb.

Example: 1 contract = verb

1 contract	4 export
2 export	5 permit
3 permit	6 contract

Listen again and repeat the sentences.

F 📼

Listen and look at how the main stress changes in these words:

□. □.
music   musician

Mark the main stress in the words below. Then listen and check your answers.

instrument / instrumental   electric /
electricity   popular / popularity
amplify / amplification   public / publicity

Music project

G

Imagine you work for a pop magazine. Interview someone you know who plays music or would like to. Ask them about:

● the instruments they play
● the style of music they play
● what music they like
● what musicians they like
● their plans and ambitions for the future

Write a report of the interview.

Stage 1 Read 'The Interview' in Lesson 37 to remind you of reporting style.
Stage 2 Plan and write paragraphs:
    1) the music the person plays
    2) musical influences/likes
    3) plans / ambitions
Stage 3 Ask another student to check your work, especially reported questions.
Stage 4 Write a final version.

H ✎

In pairs, collect all the parts of your music project. Organise them as a magazine or as a poster and display it in the classroom.

42 Revision

Language practice

A

In two teams, play noughts and crosses, with your teacher as referee. Choose a square and report the question in it. If your sentence is correct, put a nought or a cross in the square. The first team with a line wins.

'What's your name?'	'Did you watch TV last night?'	'Where are you from?'
'Have you been to New York?'	'What will you do if it rains tomorrow?'	'How long does it take you to get to school?'
'Where do they live?'	'Do you like reggae?'	'Can your sister play a musical instrument?'

B

Imagine you have been for an interview to become a member of a pop group. Write four questions that you were asked.

Example: What kind of music do you like?

In pairs, try to guess what your partner was asked.

Example: A: They asked you what your plans were.
B: No, they didn't.
A: They asked you what kind of music you liked.
B: Yes, they did.

Vocabulary

C

Copy and complete the table by making adjectives and adverbs from the nouns. Change the endings *if necessary* and add the letters below. Then check your answers in the mini-dictionary.

-al / -ally / -ful / -fully / -ous / -ously / -less / -lessly / -ive / -ively

Noun	Adjective	Adverb
emotion	. . . . .	. . . . .
music	. . . . .	. . . . .
impression	. . . . .	. . . . .
success	. . . . .	. . . . .
care	. . . . .	. . . . .
tradition	. . . . .	. . . . .
glamour	. . . . .	. . . . .

Learner training

D LEARN TO LEARN

We use special words to talk about language. Choose from the list below to describe the words in *italics* in the sentences.

noun / pronoun / adjective / adverb / verb / preposition / linking word

Example: *When* = linking word; *started* = verb;
we = pronoun; *excitedly* = adverb

1 *When* the show *started*, *we* danced *excitedly*.
2 'Rhythm and blues' *originated in cities*.
3 *She was playing* her guitar *quietly*.
4 *We* drank a *cool* fruit juice.
5 Dwayne *left* England to live *in* France, *but* he doesn't miss *it*.
6 *They had waited patiently in* the rain.

Test yourself

E

Complete the imaginary newspaper report with the words below.

were / going / terribly / stay / highly / writing /
often / answer / when / playing / if / playing /
said / very / live

Example: 1 = highly

London, 28th May 1832

Today I spoke to the ¹ . . . . .
successful composer and
violinist Signor Niccolò Paganini.
When I went into his luxurious
apartment he immediately
stopped ² . . . . . some letters and
agreed to ³ . . . . . my questions.
He was wearing black clothes
and he looked ⁴ . . . . . pale as
usual. His butler came with some
coffee and we began the
interview.

First of all, I asked him ⁵ . . . . .
he had started ⁶ . . . . . the violin.
He told me that he first
remembered ⁷ . . . . . the violin
when he was six years old.

Next I asked Signor Paganini
⁸ . . . . . he liked London. Signor
Paganini said he ⁹ . . . . . came to
London to play in concerts. He
thought the city was ¹⁰ . . . . .
beautiful and he would like to
¹¹ . . . . . here.

Then I asked Signor Paganini
what his plans for the future
¹² . . . . . He ¹³ . . . . . that he had
considered ¹⁴ . . . . . to Germany
for the summer, but finally had
decided to ¹⁵ . . . . . in Britain.

F

Do the Module check on page 107.

Do the Module check on page 107.

Language check

REPORTED QUESTIONS

'Is Dwayne Benefit your real name?'
He asked him **if** Dwayne Benefit **was his** real
name.

'When did you make your first album?'
He asked him when **he had made his** first album.

'Have you written any new songs?'
He asked him **whether he had written** any new
songs.

'When will you make your next album?'
He asked him when **he would make his** next
album.

GERUNDS AND INFINITIVES

She stopped **playing** the piano and went to bed.
While he was singing he forgot the words, so he
stopped **to look** at them.

ADVERBS

He played **brilliantly**.
He looked **really** sinister.
He **always** dressed completely in black.

91

43 The painful past

A

Match the pictures with the words below. Use the mini-dictionary to help you.

X-rays / eye tests / anaesthetics in operations / herbs / antibiotics / false teeth

(Herbs)

B

Say which of the things in exercise A were used by doctors two hundred years ago. Then read the text and check your answers.

KILL OR CURE?

Two hundred years ago in Europe, visiting the doctor was often a very painful experience. For many illnesses, doctors used to 'bleed' their patients. They used leeches, small animals which bite the skin and suck the blood. They did this because they thought
5 that illness was caused by 'bad' blood, and it was not until the nineteenth century that scientists discovered germs.

As well as bleeding patients, doctors used to give many herbal medicines, which were often more successful. However, before the discovery of penicillin, you could die if even the
10 smallest cut became infected. Also, before the nineteenth century, there were no anaesthetics. This meant that, during major operations such as having an arm or leg cut off, many people died from the shock of the pain.

If you had toothache, you would have probably gone to a
15 barber to have your tooth pulled out, as there were no dentists. Very few people had their own teeth by the time they were old, though some rich people got false teeth made for them.

Glasses were first invented by Arab and Persian doctors and many towns had shops which sold them. However, people did not
20 have their eyes tested and used to try on glasses until they found a suitable pair!

C

Read the text again and answer these questions.

1 Why did doctors bleed patients?
2 When were germs discovered?
3 Before the discovery of penicillin, what could happen if you cut yourself?
4 Why did people die during major operations?
5 What happened when people had toothache?
6 Who invented the first glasses?

Language focus:

TO HAVE / GET SOMETHING DONE

D

Match the expressions with the verbs on the right.

1 to have your tooth	a) made
2 to get false teeth	b) cut off
3 to have an arm	c) tested
4 to have your eyes	d) pulled out

Do we use these expressions to talk about something we do for ourselves or a service somebody does for us?

Did you know?

The Romans performed many difficult operations. When Julius Caesar was born, doctors operated to remove him from his mother's womb. This operation is now called a 'Caesarian'.

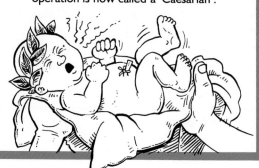

E

In pairs, look through the questionnaire. Look up any new words in the mini-dictionary. Then use the questionnaire to interview your partner.

YOUR MEDICAL HISTORY

1 Have you ever had:
  a) 'flu?
  b) mumps?
  c) chicken pox?
  d) food poisoning?
2 Have you ever broken or sprained:
  a) your leg?
  b) your ankle?
  c) your wrist?
  d) your arm?
3 Have you ever had:
  a) your eyes tested?
  b) your hearing tested?
  c) your blood tested?
4 Have you had:
  a) your tonsils taken out?
  b) your appendix taken out?
5 Have you had:
  a) a tooth taken out?
  b) any teeth filled?
  c) your teeth cleaned?
6 Have you ever had:
  a) your temperature taken?
  b) your pulse taken?
  c) your chest x-rayed?
7 Were any of these things painful?

F

Write five sentences about your partner's experiences.

Example: Fatima has had her eyes tested.

93

44 The dark side of the sun

A

In groups, decide which of these holiday activities is the most dangerous. Then tell the class what could go wrong.

mountain climbing / swimming / sunbathing / skiing / playing ball games on the beach

Example: We think mountain climbing is the most dangerous; you could fall and hurt yourself or even die.

B

Read the extract from a health shop leaflet and find out which activity *is* the most dangerous.

SUN

FRIEND OR FOE?

Nowadays, everybody is aware of the importance of a healthy life. We know all about healthy eating, healthy drinking, exercise and looking good. And after our holidays it's nice to go back to work or school with a 'healthy' suntan. But *is* it? Modern scientists now believe that out of all holiday activities, sunbathing is the most dangerous to our health.

C 🎛

Listen to the first part of the holiday programme. Copy and complete the table.

The sun's radiation	Effects
Ultra-violet A	
Ultra-violet B	
Ultra-violet C	can cause skin cancer

Language focus: QUANTITY

D

Listen to the second part of the holiday programme and complete these sentences.

INTERVIEWER:	How can we protect ourselves? With ^{1}. . . . . protection cream?
WOMAN:	You need to use ^{2}. . . . . sun protection cream. But be careful, ^{3}. . . . . creams only protect you from ultra-violet B rays, and they provide ^{4}. . . . . protection against the other rays.
INTERVIEWER:	And ^{5}. . . . . time do you recommend sunbathing? ^{6}. . . . . hours a day?
WOMAN:	If you mean lying in the sun, then ^{7}. . . . .! ^{8}. . . . . sun is bad for you. Only ^{9}. . . . . minutes on the first day. ^{10}. . . . . people return from their holiday with their skin completely ruined.

Copy and complete the table with expressions of quantity from the interview. Which do we use with countable nouns and which with uncountable nouns? Which can we use with both?

Uncountable	Countable	Countable and Uncountable
a little	*a lot of*	*some*

E

Choose five items from the list below and write how much you eat, drink or do.

Example: I eat *hardly any* meat. I drink *too much* lemonade!
I do *a lot of* walking.

meat / fish / pasta / rice / sweets / lemonade / milk / fruit / chocolate / walking / travelling by car / swimming / sunbathing

F

In groups of four, each student chooses three items from exercise E and finds out how healthy the others are.

Example:
A: How many sweets do you eat?
B: None.
C: A lot.
D: Hardly any.

G

Tell the class about one member of your group.

Example:
I think Eva is healthy because she does hardly any sunbathing, she eats plenty of fruit and she drinks a lot of milk.

H

Write an essay with the title 'Sunbathing is a dangerous holiday activity'. Plan four paragraphs:

1 introduction – different holiday activities
2 the dangers of sunbathing
3 how to sunbathe safely
4 conclusion – your opinion

45 At the doctor's

A

Read the text. Use the mini-dictionary to check any difficult words. Would you ever go to a traditional Chinese doctor?

B

Read the text again and write down:

a) the different ways a traditional Chinese doctor examines a patient.
b) the treatments that the doctor will prescribe.

Examples:
a) The doctor observes how you move, ...
b) Herbs, ...

Why do many patients now like traditional Chinese medicine?

CHINESE MEDICINE

When most doctors examine a patient, they look at the symptoms of what is wrong. Traditional Chinese doctors look at the whole person, because they believe that illness is caused by 'disharmony' within the
5 patient.

Imagine you are ill and go to a traditional Chinese doctor. As you walk into the room, the doctor observes how you move. Then the doctor looks at your tongue, which for a Chinese doctor shows the condition of your
10 heart, lungs, liver, and so on. After that the doctor asks you to describe the symptoms of your illness, and listens to the way you speak. Next, the doctor touches your skin to see if it is in good condition, and then takes six pulses, three on each wrist. These pulses
15 show different patterns of disharmony in the body, and tell the doctor what is wrong with you.

Having made the diagnosis, the doctor will prescribe herbs, acupuncture, massage or meditation, or possibly a combination of all four. Acupuncture is the most
20 spectacular treatment, when very thin needles are pushed into different parts of the body to stimulate a 'life force'.

For a long time many people were very suspicious about Chinese medicine, but now we know that it is
25 very effective in treating many kinds of illnesses. And many patients are turning to this kind of medicine, where they are treated as individuals, where the person is more important than the illness.

C

Listen to three conversations with a British doctor and complete the table.

Symptoms	Diagnosis	Treatment
1 sore throat, ... and temperature	'flu	stay in bed, aspirins, drink lots of . . . . .
2 . . . . . in ankle, can't move ankle, ankle	. . . . . ankle	. . . . . and pills
3 pain in . . . . ., being sick	appendicitis	go to hospital

What treatment do you think a Chinese doctor would have recommended?

Function focus: GOING TO THE DOCTOR'S

D

Listen again to the first conversation in exercise C and complete these sentences.

Doctor	Patient
. . . . . the matter? . . . . . me have a look at your throat. I'm . . . . . you've got 'flu. You'll . . . . . stay in bed.	. . . . . a terrible sore throat. My muscles . . . . . I . . . . . really weak.

E

In pairs, take turns to be the doctor and a patient. The patient thinks of some symptoms and then explains them to the doctor. The doctor makes a diagnosis and recommends treatment.

Pronunciation

F

Listen to ten words from this module and write them down. Then listen again and repeat them. Which words are the most difficult to pronounce?

97

A

What do you think the title of the lesson means? Read the text and find out. Use the mini-dictionary to check any difficult words.

ISLAND DOCTOR

'Marian is a doctor and a half,' said Matty Derrane. 'If she ever left these islands, we'd all be lost.'

We were riding along in Matty's horse and cart, looking at the spectacular scenery of the Aran Islands, three wild islands off the west coast of Ireland.

Matty continued saying good things about Dr Marian Broderick, who looks after the 1,500 people on the islands. 'She would do anything for you. Nothing is too much trouble.'

On her first trip to Aran, fifteen years ago, Marian fell in love with both her husband, Mairtin, and the island. Now she has been the Aran doctor for ten years. To get to the smaller islands she flies in a small plane but, in an emergency, she sometimes has to travel in the local lifeboat. Coley Hernon, 69, of the Galway lifeboat team explains: 'I've known her go out in the lifeboat, although conditions were very dangerous.'

'There are days when I think a cosy nine-to-five job would be very nice,' says Marian. 'However, I couldn't see myself either living or working in any other place. What *would* be nice would be to have someone to help with a problem once I've diagnosed it. I'd like facilities that other doctors have. There are no ambulances, no chemists and no hospital on the islands. Sometimes it would be great to have a second opinion about patients. Occasionally I phone other doctors, but they can't give an opinion on someone they can't see. Normally they play safe and say: "If you're not sure about that guy, you had better get him out of there." '

Despite the difficulties of her work, Marian and her family are happy on the island. 'I love the place. The people are open and friendly, the scenery is magnificent, and it's a good safe environment in which to bring up the kids.'

B

**Read the text again. Write T (true),
F (false) or DK (don't know).**

1 Matty thinks Marian Broderick is a
   wonderful doctor.
2 The Aran Islands are very beautiful.
3 Dr Broderick is from the islands.
4 She would prefer a nine-to-five job.
5 Next year they are opening a hospital on
   the island.
6 Marian is happy on the island.

C

Listen to a telephone call to Dr Broderick.

1 What is the problem?
2 What advice does the doctor give?

Function focus:

GIVING ADVICE AND INSTRUCTIONS

D

**Listen again to the telephone call. Copy
and complete these sentences.**

> You'd better . . .
> You should . . .

E

**Work in pairs. Student A is a country
doctor. Student B telephones with a
problem.**

B: Ask to speak to the doctor
A: Identify yourself (*Doctor . . . speaking*)
B: Identify yourself (*This is . . .*)
A: Ask: *What's the matter?*
B: Explain the problem
A: Ask about the problem (*How long . . . ?*)
B: Give more information
A: Give advice (*You'd better/You should . . .*)
B: Thank the doctor
A: Say goodbye

F

**List the advantages and disadvantages of
being a doctor in a very isolated place like
Aran.**

Examples: advantages – very quiet
           disadvantages – no hospital

G

**Write sentences comparing the advantages
and disadvantages. Use these linking
words.**

but / however / although / despite

Example: There isn't a hospital there, *but* it is
          very quiet and relaxing.

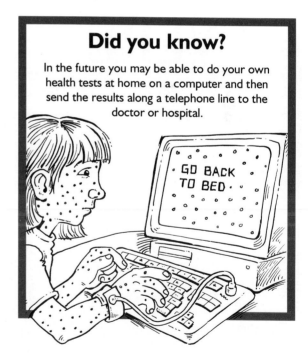

Did you know?

In the future you may be able to do your own
health tests at home on a computer and then
send the results along a telephone line to the
doctor or hospital.

GO BACK TO BED

A 🗫

In groups, make a list of everyday problems faced by the people below. Then compare your list with another group.

- people who are blind
- people who can't walk

Examples: Blind people have problems crossing the road.
People who can't walk have difficulty getting upstairs.

B

Read the text. Answer the questions with short 'yes/no' answers.

1 Is Pen y Fan a very high mountain?
2 Did Richard Kilburn climb the mountain on his own?
3 Does Sergeant Grey believe some of the climbers won't succeed?
4 Did Gail run up the mountain?

HARDER THAN EVEREST

At nearly 1,000 metres, Pen y Fan is the highest mountain in the Brecon Beacons. Not really a mountain at all. Lots of people walk up it every year, maybe strolling up
5 with their dog. But nobody has ever got up Pen y Fan like 15-year-old Richard Kilburn. He can't walk. He has climbed the first few hundred metres like a turtle, sitting on his bottom and pushing himself backwards and
10 upwards over the rocks on his hands. He has made the rest of the climb with a team of helpers. For Richard, reaching the top was a small miracle, harder than Everest.
   The miracle was shared by plenty of
15 other climbers. They are members of a climbing group from Birmingham, organised by Sergeant Grey, an ex-Royal Marine. His idea was to mix able-bodied and disabled people in climbing teams. The
20 Grey theory is simple: 'Nobody is disabled. People are just able in different ways.'
   Sergeant Grey sends his groups on five-day survival expeditions. Climbing Pen y Fan is the final challenge. Before they

25 start, he says: 'After five days with me, they will have struggled over rivers and through valleys, up hills and down again. They will have put up tents in the dark, collected river water to make tea, and prepared
30 meals from dried peas and powdered soup. They will be sweaty, tired and thirsty. At least one able-bodied member of the group will have gone home with exhaustion and won't have finished the course. Another
35 might have sprained his ankle. It will have been very hard for everyone.'
   A week later, on the last day, the different groups gather on the mountain for the final ascent. Nigel is mentally
40 handicapped and has a heart pacemaker, but he runs the last twenty metres! Gail, paralysed from the waist down, shouts: 'I got here! I did it!'
   Sergeant Grey watches it all. 'These kids
45 can do anything,' he says. 'If there's a disabled kid sitting at home who wants to climb a mountain, tell him to call me. The mountains belong to everybody.'

Language focus: FUTURE PERFECT

C

Read the text again and complete this table.

They	. . . .		struggled over rivers.
It	. . . .	have	. . . . . hard for everyone.
At least one member	won't		finished the course.
Another	. . . .		sprained his ankle.

D

Look at Sergeant Grey's plans for the last three days of the expedition. Imagine it is now the evening of Day 3. Complete the sentences below with the correct form of the verb.

> _Day 3: walk three kilometres / put up the tents / prepare a meal_
> _Day 4: cross the river / maybe climb a hill_
> _Day 5: climb Pen y Fan_

1 Today, they . . . . . three kilometres.
2 They . . . . . the tents and . . . . . a meal.
3 By tomorrow night, they . . . . . the river.
4 They . . . . . a hill, but they . . . . . Pen y Fan yet.

E

In groups, write sentences about what you think will have happened by the year 2050 in the world of disability and illness. Think about these things:

- artificial eyes
- wheelchairs that can climb stairs
- a cure for cancer
- a way to stop growing old
- robot doctors in the home
- bionic (mainly artificial) bodies
- a cure for tooth decay

Example: By the year 2050 we will have invented artificial
eyes for blind people.

F

Take turns to read out your ideas to the class. Agree and disagree.

Example:
A: We think we will have invented artificial eyes.
B: Yes, we might have.
C: We disagree. We think it's impossible.

Pronunciation

G

Listen and say how many words there are in each sentence. Remember, contractions count as two words.

Example:
1 They're going to find a way to stop growing old.
= 11

Listen again. Write down the sentences and mark the stressed words.

Example:
1 They're going to find a way to stop growing old.

Did you know?

Bionic bodies may soon be possible. Medical scientists have already developed artificial arms and legs, artificial ears, plastic heart valves and blood vessels.

48 Fluency

RADIO NORTH SEA

A 🔲
Listen to the phone-in programme and answer these questions.

1 What is the caller's problem?
2 What advice does Shulah give?

B 💬
Which things should you do when making a phone call in English, a or b?

1 First of all you should:
  a) ask who is speaking.
  b) say who you are, then give the name of the person you want to speak to.
2 When you don't understand you should:
  a) ask the person to repeat.
  b) pretend that you understand.
3 You should try to speak:
  a) as quickly as you can.
  b) slowly but clearly.
4 When telephoning for information or advice, you should finish like this:
  a) 'Thank you very much. Goodbye.'
  b) 'Thank you for calling.'

C 💬
In pairs, take turns to be the presenter of Radio North Sea and a person with a problem. Sit back to back with your partner and telephone him/her. Student A looks at number 8 on page 109. Student B looks at number 8 on page 111.

D 💬
In groups, one student is the doctor and the others are patients. Act out the situations.

- You have a horrible maths test tomorrow and you haven't studied.
- You visit the doctor and must convince him/her that you are ill.
- If you convince the doctor, you don't have to do the exam!

Pronunciation review

E 🔲 LEARN TO LEARN
Look at the list of the most common pronunciation problems. Which of them do you have?

1 Making mistakes with vowel sounds (e.g. live /ɪ/, leave /iː/).
2 Pronouncing words with lots of consonants together (e.g. prescription).
3 Getting the stress in words wrong (e.g. saying 'prescription not pre'scription).
4 Forgetting the endings of words (plurals/regular past tense endings).
5 Pronouncing letters when they should be silent (e.g. medicine /'medsən/)

Listen to a student talking about himself and his family. Write down the words he does not pronounce correctly and the number of the problem from the list above.

Example: description = problem 2

F LEARN TO LEARN
Look through your vocabulary book and choose ten words that are difficult to pronounce. Are they similar to any of the problems in exercise E?

G

Listen to another student talking. How does she try to improve her pronunciation?

Example: She marks the stress on words in her vocabulary book.

H LEARN TO LEARN

Read the letter from Alex to Shulah Allan at Radio North Sea. Grade it from 1–5 for these things:

- presentation and handwriting
- planning and paragraphs
- punctuation

KEY
5 = excellent
4 = good
3 = satisfactory
2 = bad
1 = terrible

Now find ten grammar mistakes and correct them.

I

Write a reply to Alex's letter.

Stage 1 Write down some ideas for advice.

Stage 2 Write notes for paragraphs:
1 thanking for letter
2 and 3 giving advice
4 finishing the letter

Stage 3 Look at the layout of Alex's letter (address, date, etc.).

Stage 4 Use your notes to write a reply.

Stage 5 Check your letter for mistakes.

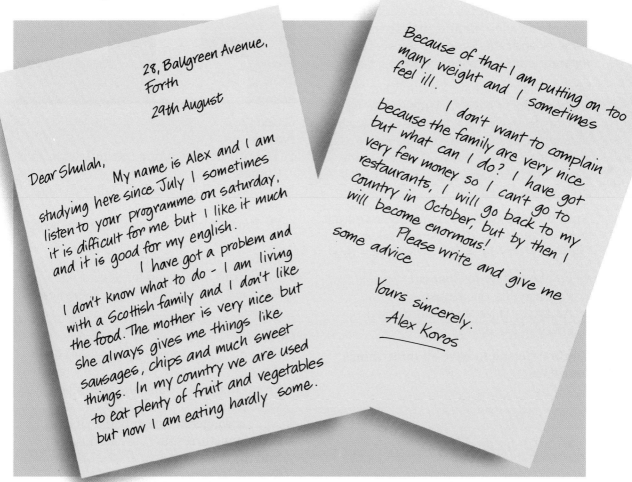

28, Ballgreen Avenue,
Forth
29th August

Dear Shulah,
My name is Alex and I am studying here since July I sometimes listen to your programme on saturday, it is difficult for me but I like it much and it is good for my english.
I have got a problem and I don't know what to do - I am living with a Scottish family and I don't like the food. The mother is very nice but she always gives me things like sausages, chips and much sweet things. In my country we are used to eat plenty of fruit and vegetables but now I am eating hardly some.

Because of that I am putting on too many weight and I sometimes feel ill.
I don't want to complain because the family are very nice but what can I do? I have got very few money so I can't go to restaurants, I will go back to my country in October, but by then I will become enormous!
Please write and give me some advice

Yours sincerely.
Alex Koros

49 Revision

Language practice

A

Tell your partner's fortune. Write predictions about what he/she will have done in fifty years' time. Then read out the predictions and see if your partner agrees.

Example: 'I think you will have become a famous artist, but you won't have made much money. I also think you will have travelled a lot to interesting places in South America and Asia. You will have got married and you might have had three or four children.'

B

Work in groups of four. Your teacher gives each of you a job: dentist, hairdresser, nurse or optician. Keep the job secret! On separate pieces of paper, write:

have my hair cut / have a tooth filled / have my eyes tested / have my temperature taken / have my teeth cleaned / have my hair washed / have my pulse taken / have some new glasses made / have my leg x-rayed / have a tooth taken out / have some contact lenses made / have my hair dyed

Next, turn the pieces of paper over and put them on the desk. Each person takes three. Find people to do things for you, like this:

A: I'd like to have my hair cut.
B: I'm sorry I'm the dentist.
A: Ah, well, I'd like my teeth cleaned.
B: OK, and I'd like . . .

The first person to have all three things done wins.

Pronunciation

C

Complete the clues below and fill in the crossword with phonetic symbols. Use the phonetic chart on page 113 and the mini-dictionary to help you.

Example: 9 across = eyes = /aɪz/

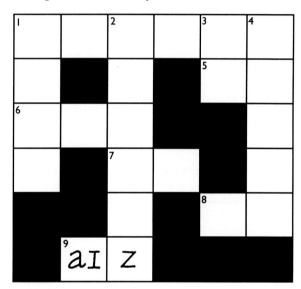

CLUES
Across
1 The title of the reading text in Lesson 45 is Chinese . . . . .
5 In Lesson 47 the climbers collected water to make . . . . .
6 Dr Broderick asked if the child had been . . . . .
7 I eat . . . . . many sweets.
8 Fresh fruit . . . . . good for you.
9 I had my . . . . . tested and got some new glasses.

Down
1 'You . . . . . take more exercise,' said the doctor.
2 I went to the . . . . . and she prescribed some pills.
3 . . . . . is dangerous to sunbathe all day.
4 In acupuncture, thin . . . . . are inserted into the body.

104

Learner training

D 🔲 LEARN TO LEARN

Look at some students' comments about revising vocabulary. Which of them help *you* remember words?

1 'Reading through my vocabulary book.'
2 'Writing sentences with examples of words.'
3 'Saying words that have the same sounds in them, like *boat* and *coat*.'
4 'Thinking about similarities between English words and words in my language, like *sugar* and *sucre*.'
5 'Associating words with topics or situations, like *food* with restaurants.'
6 'Associating words with pictures.'

Test yourself

E

Complete the text below with these words:

plenty / little / some / much / few / many / too any / any / lot

In a ¹..... of countries heart disease kills more people than ²..... other disease. But you can reduce the risks of getting it by making a ³..... simple changes to the way you live and eat.

– You should never smoke, or drink ⁴..... much alcohol.
– Make sure you take ⁵..... exercise.
– You should eat as ⁶..... fat as possible. You should not eat too ⁷..... red meat. You should also avoid eating too ⁸..... dairy products.
– You should eat ⁹..... of fresh fruit and vegetables.
– You should never cook ¹⁰..... food with fat.

F

Write the words in the correct order to make sentences.

1 a cure / by the year / may / 2020 / doctors / for cancer / found / have
2 that tooth / you / filled / should / have
3 eyes / tested / have / you'd / better / your
4 ever / have / taken out? / you / had / a tooth

G

Do the Module check on page 107.

Language check

TO HAVE / GET SOMETHING DONE

Years ago, people did not **have** their eyes **tested**.
Have you ever **had** your chest **x-rayed**?
I'm going **to get** my eyes **tested** next month.

QUANTITY

How many vegetables do you eat? **A lot.** / **A few.** / **None.**
How much fresh fruit do you eat? **A lot.** / **A little.** / **None.**
I eat **plenty of** fruit but **hardly any** meat.
She eats **too many** sweets and drinks **too much** lemonade.

FUTURE PERFECT

By the year 2050 we **will have invented** artificial eyes.
We **might / may have found** a cure for cancer.
They **won't have finished the course** because of exhaustion.

End-of-course self-evaluation

Think about how much you have learnt during the course and what you can do in English now. Look at the following areas and grade yourself, like this:

A I have no problems.
B I sometimes have difficulties.
C I have a lot of problems with this.

Speaking

☐ Use English in the class
☐ Give and find out personal information
☐ Say what I think about things, agreeing and disagreeing with people
☐ Talk about films and music
☐ Describe people and places
☐ Tell stories
☐ Give directions, instructions and advice
☐ Ask for things politely
☐ Use English in these situations: shops/travel agent's/doctor's/on the phone

Writing

☐ Make notes
☐ Make paragraph plans
☐ Check and edit my own work
☐ Assess my own and other students' written work
☐ Write personal letters
☐ Write formal letters
☐ Write stories
☐ Write film reviews
☐ Write instructions

Grammar

☐ Past tenses
☐ Present tenses
☐ Future tenses
☐ Present perfect simple/continuous
☐ Prepositions
☐ Passives
☐ Conditional sentences
☐ Articles
☐ Reported speech
☐ Adjectives and adverbs
☐ Modal verbs (*must, might*, etc.)

Study habits

☐ Use my dictionary or the mini-dictionary to get information about meaning
☐ Get information about pronunciation and stress from my dictionary
☐ Write down information about meaning, form and pronunciation in my vocabulary book
☐ Write down all the new structures we study

Listening

Give yourself a percentage (%) for how much you understand of these:

☐ Other students in class
☐ Your teacher
☐ Dialogues and conversations on the cassette
☐ Stories on the cassette
☐ Radio programmes on the cassette
☐ Pop songs
☐ Films

Reading

Give yourself a percentage (%) for how much you understand of these:

☐ Magazine or newspaper articles
☐ Extracts from fiction or poems
☐ Information texts (like encyclopedias)
☐ Tourist brochures
☐ Letters

Module check

Do this after each module. Write the answers in your notebook or in your learner diary.

1

Which was your favourite lesson in the module you've just done? Why?

Example: *Roots*, because I like music.

2

Write down two interesting or unusual facts from this module.

Example: 'Soul' music came from 'rhythm and blues' and 'gospel'.

3

Think about the speaking activities related to the Function focus spots. How good were you at doing them? Give yourself a mark out of five on the following scale:

5– I was able to communicate with no problems.
4– I had a few problems communicating, and occasionally made mistakes.
3– I had problems, but I was able to communicate what I wanted to.
2– I often made mistakes. I hesitated a lot.
1– I couldn't say anything!

4

Look at the structures in the Language check and your results in the *Test yourself* section in the Revision lesson. Give yourself a mark out of five for each structure, like this:

5– I have no problems with it and I never make mistakes.
4– I only make mistakes occasionally.
3– I sometimes have problems with it.
2– I don't understand it very well and I often make mistakes.
1– I don't understand it!

Example: Comparatives = 4

5

Read through your written work from this module. In which of the following areas do you need to improve most?

- presentation/handwriting?
- organisation/planning?
- grammar/spelling/vocabulary?

6

Look at two *listening* and two *reading* activities. Write a record of how much you understood and give yourself a percentage, like this:

100% I understood everything.
90% I understood nearly everything.
75% I understood most of it.
50% I understood it quite well.
35% I got the general idea.
10% I understood a few words.
0% I didn't understand anything.

Copy and complete the graphs below in your notebook.

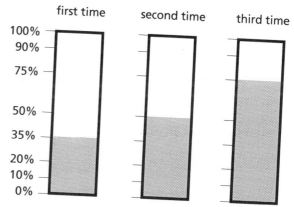

7

Look at the *Useful vocabulary* section in the Activity Book. Check you have the words in your own vocabulary book.

8

Make a list of five words with difficult sounds from this module.

PAIRWORK ACTIVITIES › A

1 (Lesson 7)

You are a top model and you meet a friend of yours in the airport. Give him/her your news and find out where he/she has been and what he/she has done recently. Use this information:

- just back from Milan (fashion show)
- recently been to Madrid, Rio and Tokyo (for fashion shows and done photo sessions for a magazine)
- going to New York and San Francisco next month

2 (Lesson 19)

Check these statements with your partner. Remember they may not be true.

Example: He went for a swim at 9 o'clock, didn't he?

JAIME PEÑAFIEL: At 9 o'clock I had a swim. Then I sat on the terrace for a few minutes. I heard someone talking to Capaldi, but I couldn't hear who it was. After that I heard the shot.

MADAME LEBRUN: I was working in the kitchen. I went to the dining room and saw the butler just before 9.30.

JIMMY CAPALDI JR: I was playing billiards in the billiard room. At about 9.25 I heard my father talking very loudly in the next room. I couldn't hear who it was.

Your partner then checks some statements with you. Use the information below which is true, to answer his/her questions.

STEPHANIE CAPALDI: sitting in summer house painting – saw someone in the library at 9.25 – with white hair

WILLIAMS: in dining room opening bottles until 9.30 – heard nothing

LADY JULIA: in breakfast room working – heard butler opening bottles – stopped at about 9.15 – then heard someone in the hall

3 (Lesson 27)

Answer your partner's questions. Do not say the name of the film star.

Born: 1925
Nationality: American
Married to actress Joanne Woodward
Appearance: blue eyes, very handsome
Hobby: motor car racing
First successful film: *The Silver Chalice* in 1954
Other films: *The Hustler* 1961 / *Butch Cassidy and the Sundance Kid* 1969 / *The Sting* 1973 / *The Color of Money* 1986
(*Answer*: Paul Newman)

Now use the cues below to ask questions to find out your partner's film star.

Example: Is it a woman? When was she born?

- Woman?   • When / born?
- Where / live?   • Who / marry?
- What / look like?   • What / first film?
- What / other successful films?
- Has / won Oscars?

Guess who your partner's star is.

4 (Lesson 29)

Ask your partner these questions. (The answers are underlined.)

1 Who was the first flight in an aeroplane made by? a) Louis Blériot b) Orville Wright c) Wilbur Wright
2 When and where was the first computer developed? a) in 1960 in Japan b) in 1957 in America   c) in 1948 in Britain
3 Where was the world's first lighthouse built? a) near Alexandria in Egypt b) near Athens in Greece c) on the coast of China
4 When was the first water closet (toilet) designed? a) in AD 100 by the Romans b) in 1320 by P. Henlein of Germany c) in 1589 by J. Harington in England

108

5 (Lesson 30)

Say to your partner: 'Bet you can't fold a piece of paper in half more than nine times!' Then give him/her these instructions:

- Take a piece of paper. Any size.
- Fold it in half evenly.
- Try to do it again eight more times.

Your partner can't do it. The number of pieces that you have to fold increases in geometrical progression: first fold = 2, second fold = 4, third fold = 8, etc. Soon you are trying to fold hundreds of pieces of paper.

6 (Lesson 32)

You are a reporter. Your partner is a singer who has recently become rich and famous. Look at the example question in exercise G, then ask your partner questions, using the following cues:

- living in a big house?
- travelling to different countries?
- giving interviews?
- having your photograph taken?
- having a lot of money?

You used to be very rich, but recently you lost all your money. Read the information below and then answer your partner's questions.

You used to drive a big, expensive car, but now you ride a bicycle and it seems strange. You had two big houses but now you live in a small flat and it's OK. When you were rich you went out a lot to parties, but now you stay at home most of the time. You haven't got enough money now to go on holiday; you travelled a lot before. You used to have a lot of friends, but now you spend a lot of time alone; you quite enjoy having this time to read books and listen to music.

7 (Lesson 34)

Describe this drawing to your partner. Your partner has to draw it.

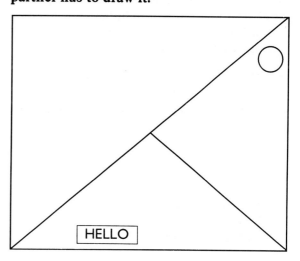

Now draw a rectangle 8 cm by 6 cm and draw what your partner describes.

8 (Lesson 48)

Phone the radio advice programme and explain your problem:

- You often get really bad headaches.
- You get a lot of homework and your parents give you extra work.
- You feel under a lot of stress.

Now you are the presenter of the radio programme. Your partner phones you and asks for advice about a problem. Ask him/her for details and then give advice.

- 'You should . . .'
- 'You'd better . . .'

B

1 (Lesson 7)

You are a top model and you meet a friend of yours in the airport. Give him/her your news and find out where he/she has been and what he/she has done recently. Use this information:

- just back from New York (photo session for television)
- recently been to Los Angeles, Atlanta and Houston (Texas) (appeared in film in Hollywood)
- going to Milan next week and Madrid the week after (to make a video)

2 (Lesson 19)

Your partner will check some statements with you. Use the information below which is true, to answer his/her questions.

JAIME PEÑAFIEL: at 9.00 had a swim – then sat on terrace – heard voices in library – Capaldi and someone who was old – heard shot

MADAME LEBRUN: was working in the kitchen – went to the dining room after 9.25 – there was nobody there

JIMMY CAPALDI JR: was playing billiards in billiard room – at 9.25 heard voices next door – father talking to somebody with a British accent

Now check these statements with your partner. Remember they may not be true.

Example: She was sitting in the summer house painting, wasn't she?

STEPHANIE CAPALDI: I was sitting in the summer house painting. At about 9.25 I saw somebody in the library with my father. I couldn't see the person.

WILLIAMS: I was in the dining room opening bottles, when I heard the shot.

LADY JULIA: I was working in the breakfast room. I could hear the butler in the next room opening bottles all evening. I didn't hear anything else.

3 (Lesson 27)

Use the cues below to ask questions to find out your partner's film star.

Example: Is it a man? / When was he born?

- Man?   • When / born?
- Nationality?   • Who / marry?
- What / look like?   • Hobbies?
- What / first film?
- What / other successful films?

Guess who your partner's star is. Then answer your partner's questions. Do not say the name of the film star.

Born: 1932 in London
Moved to California in 1939
Has been married nine times, twice to Richard Burton.
Appearance: dark hair, very beautiful
First successful film: *National Velvet* in 1944 (when she was twelve)
Other films: *Giant* (1956) / *Butterfield 8* (1960) / *Cleopatra* (1963) / *Who's Afraid of Virginia Woolf?* (1966)/ *The Mirror Cracked* (1980)
Oscars: for *Who's Afraid of Virginia Woolf?*
(Answer: Elizabeth Taylor)

4 (Lesson 29)

Ask your partner these questions. (The answers are underlined.)

1 When was the first bicycle built?
   a) 1781   b) 1823   c) <u>1839</u>
2 Who were the radioactive elements radium and polonium discovered by?
   a) <u>Marie Curie</u>   b) Albert Einstein
   c) E. Rutherford
3 When was plastic first made?
   a) <u>1862</u>   b) 1909   c) 1931
4 Where and when was the first telescope made? a) <u>in Holland in 1608</u>
   b) in Greece in 200 BC
   c) in the USA in 1808

5 (Lesson 30)

Say to your partner: 'Bet you can't tear a piece of paper into three pieces with one pull!' Now give him/her these instructions:

- Take a piece of paper. Any size.
- Fold it into thirds.
- Open it out again.
- Use some scissors to cut the paper or tear it equally along the folds, so that only 2.5 centimetres of paper keeps the strips together.
- Now hold the paper on each corner and try to tear the paper, so that the middle strip drops out.

Your partner can't do it. Paper will tear at its weakest point. It is impossible to make the two cuts exactly equal. So when you pull, the weaker one tears first.

6 (Lesson 32)

You are a singer who has recently become rich and famous. Read the information below and then answer your partner's questions.

You come from a poor family. You used to live with your parents in a small house and go on holiday once a year in England. Now you have a very big house and you travel around the world with your group. You give lots of interviews now, but you never gave any before you were famous. You have your photograph taken a lot, but you don't like it.

You are a reporter. Your partner used to be very rich, but recently has lost all his/her money. Look at the example question in exercise G, then ask your partner questions, using the following cues:

- riding a bicycle?
- living in a small flat?
- staying at home a lot?
- not having a holiday?
- being alone?

7 (Lesson 34)

Draw a rectangle 8 cm by 6 cm and draw what your partner describes.

Now describe this drawing to your partner. Your partner has to draw it.

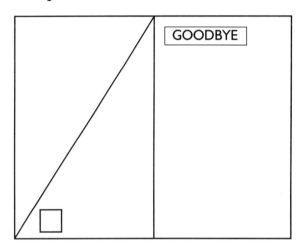

8 (Lesson 48)

You are the presenter of the radio advice programme. Your partner phones you and asks for advice about a problem. Ask him/her for details and then give advice.

- 'You should . . .'
- 'You'd better . . .'

Now phone the radio advice programme and explain your problem:

- You are going on a holiday in the sun with your parents.
- They love sunbathing but you don't – you know about the dangers.
- You think you will be bored on the holiday.

Lesson 18: Murder in Marbella

INFORMATION ABOUT THE CHARACTERS

Susan Capaldi
She didn't love her husband, who was very cruel to her.

Jimmy Capaldi Jr
He had lost a lot of money at the casino recently. When he had asked his father for more money, his father had refused.

Stephanie Capaldi
She was desperately in love with Jaime Peñafiel. Her father had told her that afternoon, that if she married Jaime she would never get any money.

Jaime Peñafiel
He had asked Mr Capaldi for permission to marry his daughter. Mr Capaldi had laughed at him and told him to come back when he was a millionaire.

Bruce Maxwell
He had found out that morning that Mr Capaldi had cheated him and that he would lose millions of dollars. He would probably go bankrupt.

Lady Julia Hamilton
She had shown her book to Mr Capaldi that day. Mr Capaldi had refused permission to publish it.

Dr Popodopolis
The old doctor loved Susan Capaldi like a daughter. He had been her family's doctor since she had been a child. He hated Capaldi.

Brigite Muller
Jimmy Capaldi had promised to divorce his wife and marry her. That evening Jimmy had changed his mind.

Madame Lebrun
Jimmy Capaldi hadn't liked lunch and he had sacked Madame Lebrun.

Williams
Williams had stolen money from the Capaldis. Mr Capaldi had just telephoned the police.

Irregular verb list

bite	bit	bitten
break	broke	broken
bring	brought	brought
build	built	built
buy	bought	bought
catch	caught	caught
choose	chose	chosen
come	came	come
cost	cost	cost
cut	cut	cut
do	did	done
draw	drew	drawn
drink	drank	drunk
drive	drove	driven
eat	ate	eaten
fall	fell	fallen
feed	fed	fed
feel	felt	felt
find	found	found
get	got	got
give	gave	given
go	went	gone
grow	grew	grown
have	had	had
hear	heard	heard
hide	hid	hidden/hid
hit	hit	hit
hold	held	held
hurt	hurt	hurt
keep	kept	kept
know	knew	known
lay	laid	laid
learn	learnt/learned	learnt/learned
leave	left	left
lose	lost	lost
make	made	made
mean	meant	meant
meet	met	met
pay	paid	paid
put	put	put
read	read	read
ride	rode	ridden
ring	rang	rung
run	ran	run
say	said	said
see	saw	seen
shoot	shot	shot
show	showed	shown/showed
sing	sang	sung

sink	sank	sunk
sit	sat	sat
sleep	slept	slept
speak	spoke	spoken
spell	spelt	spelt
spend	spent	spent
stand	stood	stood
stick	stuck	stuck
swim	swam	swum
take	took	taken
teach	taught	taught
tell	told	told
think	thought	thought
understand	understood	understood
wake (up)	woke/waked	woken/waked (up)
wear	wore	worn
win	won	won
write	wrote	written

Phonetic chart

CONSONANTS

symbol	key word
/ p /	pen
/ b /	back
/ t /	tea
/ d /	day
/ k /	key
/ g /	get
/ tʃ /	cheer
/ dʒ /	jump
/ f /	fat
/ v /	view
/ θ /	thing
/ ð /	then
/ s /	soon
/ z /	zero
/ ʃ /	fish
/ ʒ /	pleasure
/ h /	hot
/ m /	come
/ n /	sun
/ ŋ /	sung
/ l /	led
/ r /	red
/ j /	yet
/ w /	wet

VOWELS

symbol	key word
/ iː /	sheep
/ ɪ /	ship
/ e /	bed
/ æ /	bad
/ ɑː /	calm
/ ɒ /	pot
/ ɔː /	saw
/ ʊ /	put
/ uː /	boot
/ ʌ /	cut
/ ɜː /	bird
/ ə /	China

DIPHTHONGS

symbol	key word
/ eɪ /	make
/ əʊ /	note
/ aɪ /	bite
/ aʊ /	now
/ ɔɪ /	boy
/ ɪə /	here
/ eə /	there
/ ʊə /	tour

Mini-dictionary

This mini-dictionary will help you to understand all the words that are *either* important to remember *or* necessary to do the activities. Remember that you don't have to understand every word when you read a text but most words in the texts can be understood from the context.

The definitions in this mini-dictionary are taken from the **Longman New Junior English Dictionary** (1984), **Longman Active Study Dictionary** (1983) and **Longman Dictionary of Contemporary English** (1987).

We recommend that you refer to one of these dictionaries for words not included here. Remember that this mini-dictionary is not a substitute for a complete dictionary.

A

abandon /əˈbændən/ *verb* to leave or give up completely: *The baby was **abandoned** by its mother. We **abandoned** our holiday because we had no money.*

able-bodied /ˌeɪbəlˈbɒdɪd/ *adjective* physically strong and active, as opposed to being disabled

abnormal /æbˈnɔːməl/ *adjective* not **normal**, different from what is usually expected. **abnormally** /æbˈnɔːməlɪ/ *adverb*

actually /ˈæktʃuəli/ *adverb* really; in fact

adventure /ədˈventʃər/ *noun* an exciting thing that happens to someone: *He wrote a book about his **adventures** as a soldier.*

adventurous /ədˈventʃərəs/ *adjective* liking a life full of adventures

agent /ˈeɪdʒənt/ *noun* manager; a person who looks after business for someone else: *A travel **agent** arranges holidays.*

aggressive /əˈɡresɪv/ *adjective* threatening

AIDS /eɪdz/ Acquired Immune Deficiency Syndrome; a very serious disease caused by a virus which breaks down the body's natural defences against infection

air /eər/ *noun (no plural)* what we breathe: *He came by air (= in an aircraft).*

album /ˈælbəm/ *noun* 1 a book with empty pages where you can put photographs, stamps, etc. 2 a long-playing record (LP)

A level /ˈeɪ levəl/ also **advanced level** *noun* the higher of two standards of examination in Britain, needed for entrance to a university or college

alter /ˈɔːltər/ *verb* to change: *She altered her plans.* **alteration** /ˌɔːltəˈreɪʃən/ *noun*

ambition /æmˈbɪʃn/ *noun* something wished for: *Her ambition was to be a famous singer.* **ambitious** *adjective*

amorphous /əˈmɔːfəs/ *adjective* having no fixed form or shape

anaesthetic /ˌænəsˈθetɪk/ *noun* a substance that prevents the feeling of pain

analyse /ˈænəlaɪz/ *verb (present participle* **analysing**, *past* **analysed**) to find out exactly what something is made of: *The scientist **analysed** the milk and found it contained too much water.* **analysis** /əˈnæləsɪs/ *noun (plural* **analyses** /-siːz/)

ankle /ˈæŋkl/ *noun* the part of the leg just above the foot, which can bend

anorexia /ˌænəˈreksiə/ *noun* a serious illness, especially suffered by young women, in which they lose the wish for food and refuse to eat

antibiotic /ˌæntɪbaɪˈɒtɪk/ *noun* a medical substance such as penicillin, able to destroy or stop the growth of bacteria which cause disease in the body

anxiety /æŋˈzaɪətɪ/ *noun* fear and worry: *Her face was showing her **anxiety**. **anxious** /ˈæŋkʃəs/ *adjective* worried

appeal (to) /əˈpiːl/ *verb* to please, attract or interest

appendicitis /əˌpendɪˈsaɪtəs/ *noun* disease of the appendix

appendix /əˈpendɪks/ *noun* a short wormlike organ leading off the bowel, having little or no use

archaeologist /ˌɑːkɪˈɒlədʒɪst/ *noun* a person who studies very old things especially things made by man

archaeology /ˌɑːkɪˈɒlədʒɪ/ *noun (no plural)* the study of the buried remains of ancient times, such as houses, pots, tools and weapons

ascent /əˈsent/ *noun* 1 the act of going, moving or climbing up; act of rising: *We made a successful **ascent** of the mountain.* 2 a way up; upward slope, path, etc.: *a steep **ascent**, opposite **descent***

aspirin /ˈæsprɪn/ *noun* a medicine that makes pain go away

assault /əˈsɔːlt/ *verb* to attack suddenly and violently

astrology /əˈstrɒlədʒɪ/ *noun (no plural)* the study of the supposed influences on events and character of the sun, moon and stars

astronomy /əˈstrɒnəmɪ/ *noun (no plural)* the study of the sun, moon, and stars

atom /ˈætəm/ *noun* the smallest part of a substance. **atomic** /əˈtɒmɪk/ *adjective*: **Atomic** power *uses the forces in an **atom** to make power.*

avoid /əˈvɔɪd/ *verb* to get or keep away from: *Are you trying to **avoid** me?*

B

babysit /ˈbeɪbɪsɪt/ *verb* to take care of babies or children while their parents are out, especially in the evening

bankrupt /ˈbæŋkrʌpt/ *adjective* unable to pay one's debts: *The company went **bankrupt** because it couldn't sell its products.*

bandage /ˈbændɪdʒ/ *noun* a long piece of cloth used for covering a wound

barber /ˈbɑːbər/ *noun* a person who cuts men's hair

bass guitar /ˌbeɪs ɡɪˈtɑːr/ *noun* a guitar which makes the lowest sound

beautiful /ˈbjuːtɪfəl/ *adjective* very good-looking; very pleasing: *What a **beautiful** day!* **beautifully** /ˈbjuːtɪflɪ/ *adverb*

beauty /ˈbjuːtɪ/ *noun (no plural)* being beautiful: *a flower of great **beauty***

belt /belt/ *noun* a piece of cloth or leather, worn round the middle of the body: *I need a **belt** to keep up my trousers.*

biology /baɪˈɒlədʒɪ/ *noun (no plural)* the scientific study of living things

bleed /bliːd/ *verb (past **bled** /bled/)* to lose blood: *The cut on my arm **bled** for ages.*

blind /blaɪnd/ *adjective* not able to see: **blind** *in one eye* **blindness** *noun*

blond or **blonde** /blɒnd/ *noun, adjective* (a person) with light-coloured hair and skin

blood /blʌd/ the red liquid that flows round the body

blouse /blauz/ *noun* a loose garment for women, reaching from the neck to about the waist

blow /bləʊ/ *verb (past tense **blew** /bluː/, past participle **blown** /bləʊn/)* to make air go into something: *He **blew** a whistle. She **blew up** the flat tyre with a pump.*

bootlace /ˈbuːtleɪs/ *noun* a piece of string for fastening a boot

bottom /ˈbɒtəm/ *noun* the part of the body that one sits on: *He fell on his **bottom**.*

break into /breɪk ˈɪntuː/ *verb* to enter by force: *He broke into a house.*

break off /breɪk ˈɒf/ *verb* to stop

breeze /briːz/ *noun* a light wind

brilliant /ˈbrɪljənt/ *adjective* 1 very bright; shining brightly: *a **brilliant** colour* 2 very clever: *a **brilliant** student*

burglar /ˈbɜːɡlər/ *noun* a person who breaks into buildings to steal things **burglary** *noun (plural **burglaries**)*: *The police were asking questions about the **burglaries**.*

burn /bɜːn/ *verb (past **burned** /bɜːnd/ or* **burnt** /bɜːnt/) 1 to be on fire: *The house is **burning** – help!* 2 to set on fire: *We **burnt** the old furniture.*

bury /ˈberɪ/ *verb* to put a dead person into the ground

C

cable /ˈkeɪbl/ *noun* wires that carry electricity or telephone calls

calculator /ˈkælkjʊleɪtər/ *noun* a small machine which can carry out number operations and usually has a memory

calm /kɑːm/ *adjective* quiet, peaceful

cancer /ˈkænsər/ *noun* a serious illness in which a growth spreads in the body

care /keər/ *noun* 1 *(no plural)* the act of looking after a person or thing: **Take care** *of your brother while I am away.* 2 *(no plural)* thought: *When you are crossing the road, **take care**!* **careful** *adjective*: *Be **careful** when you cross the road.* **carefully** *adverb* **careless** *adjective*: **Careless** *driving causes accidents.* **carelessly** *adverb*

career /kəˈrɪər/ *noun* 1 a job for which one is trained and intends to follow for the whole of one's life 2 the general course of a person's working life

casino /kəˈsiːnəʊ/ *noun* a building used for social activities, especially playing games for money

castle /ˈkɑːsl/ *noun* a large strong building made so no one could attack the people inside

casual /'kæʒʊəl/ *adjective* **1** not planned or arranged: *a* **casual** *meeting* **2** not used for a special time or place: *He was wearing* **casual** *clothes, not his school ones*. **casually** *adverb*

CD /'si:di:/ *noun* compact disc which stores recorded music and speech

CD player /ˌsi:ˌdi: 'pleɪə^r/ *noun* an instrument which can turn the information stored on a CD back into the original music and speech

challenge /'tʃælɪndʒ/ *noun* a test of ability: *This examination is a real* **challenge**.

charge *noun* **1** a hurried attack **2** care: *I was* **in charge of** *my sister* (= I looked after her).

chest /tʃest/ *noun* the front of the body between the shoulders and the stomach

chicken pox /'tʃɪkɪn pɒks/ *noun* a disease caught especially by children, marked by a slight fever and spots on the skin

chip /tʃɪp/ *noun* **1** a small piece of fried potato **2** a very small piece of metal or plastic used in computers to store information or make the computer work. Sometimes called a **microchip**.

coast /kəʊst/ *noun* the land next to the sea: *a town on the* **coast**. **coastline** *noun: From the ship, they saw the rocky* **coastline**.

coconut /'kəʊkənʌt/ *noun* a large brown nut with a hard shell and a hollow centre filled with juice

collar /'kɒlə^r/ *noun* the part of clothes worn round the neck: *The* **collar** *of his shirt was dirty*.

colour /'kʌlə^r/ *noun* the quality that makes things look green, red, yellow, etc.: *The* **colour** *of leaves is green in summer*. **colourful** *adjective* bright; having a lot of colours: **colourful** *clothes*

combination /ˌkɒmbɪ'neɪʃn/ *noun: His character is a* **combination** *of strength and kindness*.

come /kʌm/ *(present participle* **coming** /'kʌmɪŋ/, *past tense* **came** /keɪm/, *past participle* **come**) to move towards the person speaking

come back /kʌm 'bæk/ *verb* to return: *Her parents told her to* **come back** *home before ten o'clock*.

comfort /'kʌmfət/ *noun* being free from pain, trouble, etc.: *He lived* **in comfort** (= he had enough money to live well).

comfortable /'kʌmftəbl/ *adjective: This is a very* **comfortable** *chair* (= it is nice to sit in). **comfortably** *adverb*

competition /ˌkɒmpə'tɪʃn/ *noun* a test of who is best at something: *She came first in a drawing* **competition**.

complexion /kəm'plekʃən/ *noun* the natural colour and appearance of the skin, especially of the face

compose /kəm'pəʊz/ *verb (present participle* **composing**, *past* **composed**) to write or make up: *to* **compose** *songs and music* **composer** *noun* a person who composes

conceal /kən'si:l/ *verb* to hide

concentrate /'kɒnsəntreɪt/ *verb* to keep your thoughts or attention on one thing: *Are you* **concentrating on** *your work?*

conch /kɒntʃ/ *noun* a large twisted sea shell

confess /kən'fes/ *verb* to tell about the things you have done wrong: *When the police questioned the man, he* **confessed**.

confession /kən'feʃn/ *noun: He made a* **confession**.

constable /'kʌnstəbəl/ *noun* a British policeman of the lowest rank

consider /kən'sɪdə^r/ *verb* to think about: *I'm* **considering** *changing my job*.

consideration /kənˌsɪdə'reɪʃən/ *noun (no plural)* They gave the plan careful **consideration** (= thought). *She shows great* **consideration** *to* (= cares about the wishes of) *her parents*.

contact lens /'kɒntækt lens/ *noun* a very small curved piece of glass or plastic which fits closely over the eye to improve the eyesight

contract /'kɒntrækt/ *noun* a written agreement to do work or sell goods at an agreed price

contract /kən'trækt/ *verb* **1** to become smaller: *Metal* **contracts** *as it cools*. **2** to arrange by formal agreement: *He was* **contracted** *to give a concert in Paris*. **3** to get an illness: *My son* **contracted** *flu*.

conventional /kən'venʃənəl/ *adjective* following accepted customs and standards

convict /kən'vɪkt/ *verb* to decide in a law court that somebody is guilty of a crime: *He was* **convicted** *of stealing*.

cool /ku:l/ *adjective* **1** not warm, but not very cold: *The room was* **cool** *after the sun had gone down*. **2** calm: *Don't get excited about the examination; keep* **cool**. **3** fashionable: *His hairstyle is really* **cool**.

coral /'kɒrəl/ *noun* a white, pink or reddish hard substance formed from the bones of very small sea animals. It is often used for making jewellery: *a* **coral** *necklace*

cosmetics /kɒz'metɪks/ *plural noun* substances put on the skin, especially of the face, and on the hair to make them look prettier

costume /'kɒstju:m/ *noun* clothes worn for a special reason, or to represent a country or time in history: *Her* **national costume** *showed which country she came from*.

cottage /'kɒtɪdʒ/ *noun* a small house in the country

course /kɔ:s/ *noun* a set of lessons: *What* **course** *are you taking at college?*

court /kɔ:t/ *noun* a place where someone is questioned about a crime, and where people decide whether he is guilty or not

cover *noun* something that is put over something else: *The book had a blue* **cover**.

crepe-soled shoes /'kreɪpsəʊld ʃu:z/ *noun* shoes with the bottoms made of a soft tightly pressed rubber, **crepe rubber**

crew /kru:/ *noun* **1** a group of people working together, especially in films or the theatre **2** all the people working on a ship or plane

crisis /'kraɪsɪs/ *noun* **crises** *(plural)* a turning point in the course of something; moment of great danger, difficulty or uncertainty: *Their friendship came to a* **crisis** *because he had to go abroad*.

cruel /'kru:əl/ *adjective* liking to hurt other people or animals: *He is* **cruel** *to animals*. **cruelty** *noun (no plural)*: **cruelty** *to animals*

cruise /kru:z/ *noun* a trip on the sea for pleasure

culture /'kʌltʃə^r/ *noun* the way of life of a group of people: *These two countries have different* **cultures**.

cure /kjʊə^r/ *verb (present participle* **curing**, *past* **cured**) to make someone better when they have been ill: *I hope the doctor can* **cure** *the pain in my shoulder*.

cure /kjʊə^r/ *noun* a way of making better: *a* **cure** *for an illness*

curl /kɜ:l/ *noun* a roll or round shape: *Her hair was in* **curls**. **curly** *adjective* (**curlier, curliest**): **curly** *hair*

customs /'kʌstəmz/ *plural noun* a department of the government that controls what is brought into a country

customs officer /'kʌstəmz ˌɒfɪsə^r/ *noun* At the airport a **customs officer** searched his case.

cut /kʌt/ *verb (present participle* **cutting**, *past* **cut**) to break with a knife or blade: *He* **cut** *the apple in half. He has* **cut** *his leg, and it is bleeding. She* **cut** *her hair* (= made it shorter).

cut off /kʌt 'ɒf/ to separate by cutting: *Please* **cut off** *a piece of cheese*.

D

damage /'dæmɪdʒ/ *verb (present participle* **damaging**, *past* **damaged**) to hurt; cause damage to: *The cars were badly* **damaged** *in the accident*.

danger /'deɪndʒə^r/ *noun* **1** *(no plural)* the possibility of loss or harm: *There is always* **danger** *(of floods) in a storm. He put his life* **in danger** *when he ran across the busy street*. **2** something that causes danger: *the* **danger** *of smoking*. **dangerous** /'deɪndʒərəs/ *adjective: a* **dangerous** *bend in the road*

data /'deɪtə/ *noun* information: *We keep the* **data** *in our files*.

decay /dɪ'keɪ/ *noun (no plural)* the state of being bad: *tooth* **decay**

decay /dɪ'keɪ/ *verb* to go bad: *His teeth had* **decayed**, *because he had never cleaned them*.

deduce /dɪ'dju:s/ *verb* to decide something about a situation by using discovered knowledge: *He had not been seen for three weeks and she* **deduced** *that he was dead*. **deduction** /dɪ'dʌkʃən/ *noun*

defiance /dɪ'faɪəns/ *noun* showing no fear or respect; refusal to obey

defy /dɪ'faɪ/ *verb (present participle* **defying**, *past* **defied** /dɪ'faɪd/) to be ready to fight against; show no respect for: *He* **defied** *his mother and didn't go to school*. **defiant** /dɪ'faɪənt/ *adjective*

delicate /'delɪkət/ *adjective* fine; easily harmed or broken: *a* **delicate** *glass/a* **delicate** *child who is often ill*. **delicately** /'delɪkətlɪ/ *adverb*

democracy /dɪ'mɒkrəsɪ/ *noun* a government or country where everyone has an equal right to choose their leaders, by voting. **democratic** /ˌdemə'krætɪk/ *adjective*

dense /dens/ *adjective* thick: **dense** *forest*

depress /dɪ'pres/ *verb* to make someone feel sad: *He was* **depressed** *because he had not passed his examinations*.

depression /dɪ'preʃn/ *noun (no plural)* feeling sad: *A holiday will help his* **depression**.

desperate /'despərət/ *adjective* ready to do anything to get what you want: *The man lost in the desert was* **desperate** *for water*. **desperately** *adverb*

diagnose /'daɪəgnəʊz/ *verb* to discover the nature of a disease.

diagnosis /ˌdaɪəg'nəʊsɪs/ *noun* the statement which is the result of diagnosing: *The doctor will give me the* **diagnosis** *next week.*

dig /dɪg/ *verb* (*present participle* **digging**, *past* **dug** /dʌg/) to cut downwards into something: *He is* **digging** *in his garden.*

direction /də'rekʃən/ *noun* where someone or something is going or pointing; the way: *In which* **direction** *are you going, north or south?* **direct** /daɪ'rekt/ *verb* to tell someone the way to go or what to do

director /də'rektər/ *noun* a person who directs a play or film, telling actors, cameramen, etc. what to do

disability /ˌdɪsə'bɪlɪtɪ/ *noun* the state of being disabled: *He played the piano well even though he had a hearing* **disability**.

disabled /dɪs'eɪbəld/ *adjective* not being able to move your body easily because of some illness or wound: *The* **disabled** *man could not use the stairs. Blind people and deaf people are* **disabled** *too.*

disaster /dɪ'zɑːstər/ *noun* something very bad, especially something that happens to a lot of people: *The floods were a* **disaster**, *hundreds of people were killed and crops destroyed.* **disastrous** /dɪ'zɑːstrəs/ *adjective*: *a* **disastrous** *mistake*

disk /dɪsk/ *noun* a round flat record which stores information in a computer

disease /dɪ'ziːz/ *noun* illness: *a* **disease** *of the eyes*

disharmony /dɪs'hɑːmənɪ/ *noun* opposite of **harmony**

distinctive /dɪ'stɪŋktɪv/ *adjective* clearly marking a person or thing as different from others: *a* **distinctive** *appearance*

divorce /dɪ'vɔːs/ *verb* (*present participle* **divorcing** *past* **divorced**) to arrange by law for a husband and wife to separate, so that either may marry again: *"When did she* **divorce** *her husband?" "They got* **divorced** *last year."*

dose /dəʊs/ *noun* an amount of medicine that you should take at one time: *Here is your medicine — the* **dose** *is two spoonfuls every four hours.*

drainpipe trousers /ˌdreɪnpaɪp 'traʊzəz/ *plural noun* a fashion for a piece of clothing which covers the lower part of the body and legs, where the leg parts are like narrow tubes or pipes

drop off /drɒp 'ɒf/ *verb* to fall asleep: *She dropped off because the lesson was so boring.*

drop out /drɒp'aʊt/ *verb* to fall from: *The letter dropped out of my pocket when I took my jacket off.*

drum /drʌm/ *noun* 1 a musical instrument made of a round hollow box with skin stretched tightly over it, which is beaten

dye /daɪ/ *verb* (*present participle* **dyeing**, *past* **dyed** /daɪd/) to give a colour to: *She* **dyed** *her hair black.*

E

eager /'iːgər/ *adjective* very anxious to do something: *The boy was* **eager** *to show me his stamps.* **eagerly** /'iːgəlɪ/ *adverb*

earn /ɜːn/ *verb* to get money in return for work you do: *He has* **earned** *a lot of money by working in the evenings.*

earring /'ɪəˌrɪŋ/ *noun* an ornament worn in or on the ear

ecologist /ɪ'kɒlədʒɪst/ *noun* someone who studies the pattern of natural relations of plants, animals and people to each other and to their surroundings

effective /ɪ'fektɪv/ *adjective* getting the result you want: *The medicine is an* **effective** *cure for a headache.*

efficient /ɪ'fɪʃnt/ *adjective* working well and getting a lot of things done

electricity /ˌɪlek'trɪsətɪ/ *noun* (*no plural*) power for lighting, heating, machinery, etc. that is sent through wires: *Do you use* **electricity** *for cooking?* **electric** /ɪ'lektrɪk/ *adjective* working by electricity: *an* **electric** *guitar.* **electrical** *adjective* about electricity: *The cooker isn't working because of an* **electrical** *fault.* **electrician** /ˌɪlək'trɪʃn/ *noun*: *An* **electrician** *repaired the cooker*

emergency /ɪ'mɜːdʒənsɪ/ *noun* (*plural* **emergencies**) a sudden happening that needs something done about it all at once: *The hospital has to treat* **emergencies** *such as car accidents. In an* **emergency**, *telephone the police.*

emotional /ɪ'məʊʃənəl/ *adjective* (of words, music, etc.) having or causing strong feeling

endanger /ɪn'deɪndʒər/ *verb* to cause danger to. **endangered** *adjective* describes things, especially animals, which are in danger of dying out: **endangered** *species*

enjoy /ɪn'dʒɔɪ/ *verb* to get pleasure from: *I* **enjoy** *my job.* **enjoyable** *adjective*: *My job is* **enjoyable**. **enjoyment** *noun* (*no plural*): *I get a lot of* **enjoyment** *from my job.*

evil /'iːvl/ *adjective* very bad: *It was* **evil** *to kill the old woman and steal all her money.*

excellent /'eksələnt/ *adjective* very good

excite /ɪk'saɪt/ *verb* (*present participle* **exciting**, *past* **excited**) to give strong and pleasant feelings; cause to lose calmness: *The games* **excited** *the children and they all started to shout.* **excited** *adjective* having strong and pleasant feelings; not calm

excitement /ɪk'saɪtmənt/ *noun*: *The* **excitement** *of the games has made them tired.* **exciting** *adjective* able to make someone excited: **exciting** *news*

exhaustion /ɪg'zɔːstjən/ *noun* a state of extreme tiredness. **exhaust** /ɪg'zɔːst/ *verb* to make very tired

expedition /ˌekspə'dɪʃn/ *noun* a journey, usually a long one to find out something: *an* **expedition** *to find the beginning of the River Nile*

experience /ɪk'spɪərɪəns/ *noun* something that happens to you

expert /'ekspɜːt/ *noun* a person who is very good at something special: *an* **expert** *in cookery/a cookery* **expert**

explore /ɪk'splɔːr/ *verb* (*present participle* **exploring**, *past* **explored**) to find out about a place by going and looking: *Have you really* **explored** *your nearest town?* **exploration** /ˌeksplə'reɪʃn/ *noun*

export /ɪk'spɔːt/ *verb* to send something out of the country to be sold abroad: *South Africa* **exports** *fruit.*

export /'ekspɔːt/ *noun* something that is exported: *Fruit is one of South Africa's* **exports**.

extravagant /ɪk'strævəgənt/ *adjective* spending too much money: *She's very* **extravagant** *– she spends all her money on clothes.* **extravagance** *noun*

eye test /'aɪ test/ *noun* examination of the eyes and their power to see

F

fact-file /'fæktfaɪl/ *noun* a collection of the information on a particular subject

fade /feɪd/ *verb*, *present participle* **fading**, *past* **faded** to lose colour or brightness: *If you leave that dress in the sun it will* **fade**.

fantastic /fæn'tæstɪk/ *adjective* very good, wonderful, magnificent

fantasy /'fæntəsɪ/ *noun* something made by the imagination

fashion /'fæʃn/ *noun* the way of dressing or doing something that is considered best at one time: *Is it the* **fashion** *to wear short skirts? Yes, short skirts are* **in fashion**. **fashionable** /'fæʃnəbl/ *adjective*: *Short skirts are* **fashionable** *now.* **fashionably** *adverb*

fat /fæt/ *noun* (*no plural*) an oily substance, especially the oil that comes from meat when it is cooked: *Cakes are made of* **fat** *and flour.*

ferry /'ferɪ/ *noun* (*plural* **ferries**) a boat that takes people or things across water: *A* **ferry** *crosses the river every hour.*

fetch /fetʃ/ *verb* to go somewhere and bring something back: *Will you* **fetch** *my coat?*

fill /fɪl/ *verb* to put a special material into a hole in a tooth to preserve it. **filling** /'fɪlɪŋ/ *noun*

financial /faɪ'nænʃl/ *adjective*: connected with money: *The bank gave him* **financial** *advice.* **financially** *adverb*

fine /faɪn/ *noun* money paid as a punishment: *to pay a* **fine** *of £100*

fine /faɪn/ *verb* (*present participle* **fining**, *past* **fined**) to make someone pay a fine: *The man was* **fined** *£100.*

fit /fɪt/ *verb* (*present participle* **fitting**, *past* **fitted**) to be the right size for: *The trousers don't* **fit** *him, they are too small.*

flared /fleəd/ *adjective* (of trousers or a skirt) shaped to get wider towards the bottom

flick /flɪk/ *verb* to move with a light quick blow: *The cow* **flicked** *the flies away with its tail.*

flight /flaɪt/ *noun* flying: *The (plane)* **flight** *took three hours. He saw the birds* **in flight**.

flu /fluː/ *noun* short name for the illness **influenza**

fluorescent /fluə'resənt/ *adjective* (of a substance) having the quality of giving out bright white light when electric or other waves are passed through

fold /fəʊld/ *verb* to turn part of something over the other part: *She* **folded** *the letter so that it would fit into her bag.*

fond /fɒnd/ *adjective* loving: *She has* **fond** *parents. I am not* **fond of** *(= I do not like) eating meat.*

food poisoning /ˈfuːd ˌpɔɪsnɪŋ/ *noun* an illness in which harmful substances have got into the body from bad food

fork /fɔːk/ *noun* an instrument with a handle and two or more points at the end: *We use a* **fork** *to eat food. A big* **fork** *is used to dig the earth.*

formal /ˈfɔːml/ *adjective* according to accepted rules or customs: *You must wear* **formal** *dress for the dinner.*

fort /fɔːt/ *noun* a strong place which can protect the people inside from attack

friction /ˈfrɪkʃən/ *noun* 1 the natural force which tries to stop one surface sliding over another 2 the repeated rubbing of two surfaces together

friendly /ˈfrendli/ *adjective*: kind and helpful: *He is* **friendly** *to us all.*

funny /ˈfʌni/ *adjective* (**funnier, funniest**) 1 making you laugh; amusing: *a funny joke* 2 strange; unusual: *I had a* **funny** *feeling you would come. What's that* **funny** *smell?*

fur /fɜːr/ *noun* (*no plural*) the soft hair on some animals: *Cats have* **fur**.

G

gambler /ˈgæmblər/ *noun* someone who tries to win money on horse races, games, cards, etc.

gather /ˈgæðər/ *verb* to bring together: *They* **gathered** *in the square at six o'clock.*

genetic code /dʒəˌnetɪk ˈkəʊd/ *noun* the arrangement of genes which controls the way a living thing develops

geology /dʒɪˈɒlədʒɪ/ *noun* (*no plural*) the study of rocks, and how they were made

germ /dʒɜːm/ *noun* a very small piece of living substance that can grow in animals or people, often giving them an illness

get /get/ *verb* (*present participle* **getting**, *past* **got** /gɒt/) 1 to receive or obtain: *I got a letter today.* 2 to have or possess: *I have* **got** *a dog.* 3 to catch an illness: *I* **got** *flu last week.* 4 to arrive: *When we* **got** *to the station the train was waiting.*

get away *verb* to escape, e.g. from the scene of a crime: *The thieves* **got away** *with the money.*

get back *verb* to return, especially to one's home: *When did you* **get back** *from school?*

get on *verb* to do well, succeed: *He wanted to* **get on** *at school so he could go to university.*

glamour /ˈglæmər/ *noun* a special quality of charm and beauty; attractiveness: *She added a touch of* **glamour** *by wearing a beautiful dress.* **glamorous** /ˈglæmərəs/ *adjective* having glamour **glamorously** /ˈglæmərəslɪ/ *adverb*

glorious /ˈglɔːrɪəs/ *adjective* very beautiful: *Isn't it a* **glorious** *day?*

go /gəʊ/ *verb* (*present participle* **going** /ˈgəʊɪŋ/, *past tense* **went** /went/, *past participle* **gone** /gɒn/) to move: *Are you* **going** *to school today?*

go on *verb* to continue: **Go on** *with your work.*

go with *verb* to match: *Mary's blue dress* **goes with** *her shoes.*

goodie /ˈgʊdɪ/ *noun* a good person or hero

gospel /ˈgɒspəl/ *noun* a style of popular music usually performed by black American singers in which religious songs are sung strongly and loudly

gravity /ˈgrævətɪ/ *noun* (*no plural*) the force which brings things down to Earth: *When you let go of something,* **gravity** *makes it fall to the floor.*

guy /gaɪ/ *noun* a man, fellow: *a nice* **guy**

H

hamster /ˈhæmstər/ *noun* a small animal with pockets in its cheeks for storing food, kept as a pet

handicapped /ˈhændɪkæpt/ *adjective* having a disability of the body or mind

handsome /ˈhænsəm/ *adjective* nice to look at (usually used of men)

hang /hæŋ/ *verb* 1 (*past* **hung** /hʌŋ/) to fasten something at the top so that the lower part is free: *I* **hung** *my coat* (**up**) *on a hook.* 2 (*past* **hanged**) to kill, usually as a punishment, by holding someone above the ground with a rope around his neck

harmony /ˈhɑːmənɪ/ *noun* 1 notes of music combined in a pleasant sounding way 2 a state of agreement in feeling, ideas, etc.; peacefulness: *My cat and dog live together in perfect* **harmony**.

headache /ˈhedeɪk/ *noun* a pain in the head

hearse /hɜːs/ *noun* a car which is used to carry a body in a coffin to the funeral

heart /hɑːt/ *noun* the part of your body in your chest that pumps the blood round the body

heat /hiːt/ *noun* (*no plural*) the feeling of something hot: *The* **heat** *of the sun made her feel ill.*

heavy /ˈhevɪ/ *adjective* (**heavier, heaviest**) 1 weighing a lot: *How* **heavy** *was the baby when he was born? We had* **heavy** (= a large amount of) *rain today.* **Heavy** *lorries can damage roads and buildings.* 2 a style of music which is loud and aggressive

hedge /hedʒ/ *noun* small trees between fields or along roads making a wall

herb /hɜːb/ *noun* any plant used for medicine or for giving a special taste to food. **herbal** /ˈhɜːbəl/ *adjective*

hill /hɪl/ *noun* a piece of ground higher than usual; small mountain: *I climbed up the* **hill** *and ran down the other side; I had to go slowly* **uphill**, *but I could run* **downhill**.

hole /həʊl/ *noun* an empty space or opening in something: *I fell into a* **hole** *in the road.*

hospitable /hɒˈspɪtəbəl/ *adjective* showing welcome and kindness to visitors

household name /ˌhaʊshəʊld ˈneɪm/ *noun* a person known and spoken of by almost everybody

hug /hʌg/ *verb* (*present participle* **hugging**, *past* **hugged**) to put the arms round someone and hold them: *He* **hugged** *his son.*

hunter /ˈhʌntər/ *noun* a person who hunts animals or birds

I

ideal /aɪˈdɪəl/ *adjective* the best possible: *This book is* **ideal** *— it's exactly what I needed.*

illegal /ɪˈliːgl/ *adjective* not allowed by law: *It is* **illegal** *to steal things.*

image /ˈɪmɪdʒ/ *noun* 1 a picture in the mind, or in a mirror: *He saw the* **image** *of his face in the mirror.* 2 the opinion which others have of one: *He will have to improve his* **image** *if he wants to be chosen.*

imitate /ˈɪmɪteɪt/ *verb* (*present participle* **imitating**, *past* **imitated**) to copy: *She* **imitated** *the way her teacher talked.* **imitation** /ɪmɪˈteɪʃən/ *noun*

imperfect /ɪmˈpɜːfɪkt/ *adjective* not perfect; faulty: *an* **imperfect** *knowledge of English*

impossible /ɪmˈpɒsəbl/ *adjective* not possible; not able to happen: *I can't come today; it's* **impossible**. **im'possibly** *adverb: That sum looks* **impossibly** *difficult.*

impressive /ɪmˈpresɪv/ *adjective*: causing strong feelings or thought: *His work was very* **impressive**.

in /ɪn/ *adverb* fashionable; liked and worn a lot: *Those kind of trousers are* **in** *this year.*

incredible /ɪnˈkredəbəl/ *adjective* too strange to be believed

incredibly /ɪnˈkredəblɪ/ *adverb* very; extremely

independent /ˌɪndɪˈpendənt/ *adjective* able to look after yourself; not governed by anyone or anything else: *Although she is young, she is very* **independent**. *America has not always been* **independent**.

inefficient /ˌɪnɪˈfɪʃənt/ *adjective* not efficient; not working well so as to produce good results quickly

inexpensive /ˌɪnɪkˈspensɪv/ *adjective* not expensive; cheap; low in price

informal /ɪnˈfɔːml/ *adjective* happening or done in an easy way, not according to rules: *It's an* **informal** *party so you can wear what you like.* **informally** *adverb*

inhabited /ɪnˈhæbɪtɪd/ *adjective* lived in

instruction /ɪnˈstrʌkʃən/ *noun* teaching or advice on how to do something: *Read the* **instructions** *on the packet.*

instrument /ˈɪnstrəmənt/ *noun* 1 a tool used for doing something special: *A pen is an* **instrument** *for writing.* 2 an object which is played to give musical sounds: *A piano is a* **musical instrument**.

instrumental /ˌɪnstrəˈmentəl/ *adjective* (of music) for instruments, not voices

insurance /ɪnˈʃʊərəns/ *noun* (*no plural*) money paid to a company which will pay a large amount if you are in an accident, die, etc.

invention /ɪnˈvenʃən/ *noun* something made, thought of or produced for the first time: *the* **invention** *of the telephone*

isolate /ˈaɪsəleɪt/ *verb* (*present participle* **isolating**, *past* **isolated**) to separate; set apart from other things or people

ivory /ˈaɪvərɪ/ *noun* (*no plural*) hard, yellowish-white substance taken from the tusks (= long teeth) of elephants

J

jangle /'dʒæŋgəl/ *noun* a hard sound of metal striking against metal

jersey /'dʒɜːzɪ/ *noun* a piece of clothing, usually made of wool, that covers the top part of the body. **Sweater** and **jumper** are other words for **jersey**.

jet /dʒet/ *verb* to travel by jet aircraft

jewellery /'dʒuːəlrɪ/ *noun* (no plural) jewels, gold, etc. made into rings, earrings, and other ornaments

K

keen /kiːn/ *adjective* eager to do something; liking to do something: *He was* **keen** *to see the new film. Are you* **keen** *on swimming? – Yes, I like it very much.* **keenly** *adverb*

keep up with /kiːp ʌp wɪð/ *verb* to remain level

keyboard /'kiːbɔːd/ *noun* a row of keys on a musical instrument or a machine: *the* **keyboard** *of a piano/computer*

kilt /kɪlt/ *noun* a short skirt with many pressed folds worn usually by Scotsmen

kimono /kɪ'məʊnəʊ/ *noun* a long coatlike garment worn in Japan by women

L

lack /læk/ *noun* too little of something: *We have a great* **lack** *of water; there has been no rain.*

lamb /læm/ *noun* a young sheep

law /lɔː/ *noun* a rule made by the government that all people must obey: *There is a* **law** *to stop people driving too fast in towns. It is* **against the law** *(= not allowed by the law) to steal.* **lawful** *adjective: It is not* **lawful** *to steal.*

lawyer /'lɔːjər/ *noun* a person who has studied the laws of our country and helps us to understand them

lead /liːd/ *noun* the chief person in a film, a musical group or orchestra

leather /'leðər/ *noun* (no plural) the skin of a dead animal specially prepared for use: **leather** *shoes*

legal /'liːgl/ *adjective* allowed by the law: *Stealing is not* **legal.**

let go /let 'gəʊ/ *verb* to stop holding something

lifeboat /'laɪfbəʊt/ *noun* a boat used for saving people in danger at sea

lift /lɪft/ *verb* to rise into the air

lighting engineer /,laɪtɪŋ endʒə'nɪər/ *noun* a person who is trained to control the lights for concerts, theatres or films

liquid /'lɪkwɪd/ *noun* a thing like water or milk that can be poured. **liquid** *adjective*

literacy /'lɪtərəsɪ/ *noun* the state of being able to read and write

liver /'lɪvər/ *noun* a large part inside the body which cleans the blood

lobster /'lɒbstər/ *noun* a sea animal with a shell, a tail, and ten legs

look /lʊk/ *verb* to point the eyes towards a thing to try to see it: *The teacher told us to* **look** *at the blackboard.*

look for *verb* to try to find

look through *verb* to examine, especially for points to be noted

love affair /'lʌv ə,feər/ *noun* an experience of love between two people

luck /lʌk/ *noun* (no plural) the good and bad things that happen to you by chance: *It was good* **luck** *that I met you here; I did not expect to see you.* **lucky** *adjective* (**luckier, luckiest**) having or bringing good luck: *I was* **lucky** *that I met you here. Some people think that black cats are* **lucky** *(= bring good luck).*

lung /lʌŋ/ *noun* one of the two parts inside the chest with which we breathe

luxury /'lʌkʃərɪ/ *noun* 1 (no plural) great comfort: *They live* **in luxury** *in a very big house.* 2 (plural **luxuries**) something that you do not really need, but that is very pleasant: *Going to school in a car is a* **luxury.** **luxurious** /lʌg'zʊərɪəs/ *adjective* fine and expensive; very comfortable: *a* **luxurious** *hotel*

M

magnificent /mæg'nɪfɪsənt/ *adjective* great, grand, etc.: *a* **magnificent** *birthday party*

manager /'mænɪdʒər/ *noun* a person who looks after a business, a sports team, a singer, etc.

mansion /'mænʃən/ *noun* a large house, usually belonging to a wealthy person

mashed potato /,mæʃt pə'teɪtəʊ/ *noun* potato crushed with milk and butter until it is soft

massage /'mæsɑːʒ/ *noun* treatment of the body by pressing and rubbing one's hands on it to take away pain or stiffness. **massage** *verb*

measure /'meʒər/ *verb* (present participle **measuring**, past **measured**) to find out the size, weight, or amount of anything: *Mother* **measured** *me to see what size of dress I should have.* **measurement** /'meʒəmənt/ *noun*

meditation /,medɪ'teɪʃən/ *noun* thinking seriously or deeply

mental arithmetic /,mentl ə'rɪθmətɪk/ *noun* (no plural) work with numbers done only in the mind, not by writing

mess around /,mes ə'raʊnd/ *verb* to spend time doing things with no speed or plan, but according to one's feelings at the time

milk float /'mɪlk fləʊt/ *noun* a vehicle used by a milkman for delivering milk

minimum /'mɪnɪməm/ *noun* the smallest possible amount, number, or size: *You must get a* **minimum** *of 40 questions right to pass the examination.*

minimum /'mɪnɪməm/ *adjective* smallest: *The* **minimum** *pass mark in the examination is 40 out of 100.*

mini-skirt /'mɪnɪskɜːt/ *noun* a type of very short skirt

miracle /'mɪrəkl/ *noun* a wonderful happening which cannot be explained so is thought to be caused by God **miraculous** /mɪ'rækjʊləs/ *adjective: a* **miraculous** *cure for an illness* **miraculously** *adverb*

model /'mɒdl/ *noun* a person, especially a young woman, who models clothes: *a fashion* **model**

modest /'mɒdɪst/ *adjective* not making oneself noticed or telling people about what you do well: *She is very* **modest** *about the prizes she has won.* **modesty** *noun* (no plural)

mood /muːd/ *noun* the way we feel at any one time: *The beautiful sunny morning put me in a happy* **mood.**

motive /'məʊtɪv/ *noun* the reason for doing something: *His* **motive** *for working so hard is that he needs money.*

movies /'muːvɪz/ *noun* American English for the cinema

mug /mʌg/ *verb* to rob with violence especially in a dark street. **mugging** /'mʌgɪŋ/ *noun*

mug /mʌg/ *noun* a kind of cup with a flat bottom, straight sides and handle but with no saucer

mumps /mʌmps/ *noun* (no plural) an illness which causes fever and swellings in the neck and throat

murder /'mɜːdər/ *verb* to kill a person when you have decided to do it. **murderer** *noun* a person who murders someone

murder /'mɜːdər/ *noun* an act of murdering: **Murder** *is a serious crime.*

muscle /'mʌsl/ *noun* one of the pieces of stretchy material in the body which can tighten to move parts of the body: *We use our* **muscles** *to bend our arms and legs.*

music /'mjuːzɪk/ *noun* (no plural) 1 the pleasant sounds made by voices or by instruments: *to listen to* **music** 2 a written or printed set of musical notes: *a* **sheet of music.** **musical** *adjective* of music; skilled in music: *She is very* **musical.** *She plays and sings well.* **musically** *adverb*

mystery /'mɪstərɪ/ *noun* (plural **mysteries**) a strange thing which we cannot explain: *Who had taken the money? It was a* **mystery.** **mysterious** /mɪ'stɪərɪəs/ *adjective*

N

needle /'niːdl/ *noun* a thin piece of very sharp pointed metal

nervous /'nɜːvəs/ *adjective* afraid: *The old woman felt* **nervous** *as she tried to cross the busy road.* **nervously** *adverb*

nine-to-five job /,naɪn tə 'faɪv dʒɒb/ *noun* paid employment with regular hours of work, especially in an office

noise /nɔɪz/ *noun* a loud sound, often unpleasant: *Planes make a lot of* **noise.** *My car's making strange* **noises.** **noisily** *adverb* **noisy** *adjective* (**noisier, noisiest**): *'What a* **noisy** *class you are!' said the teacher.*

nuclear fission /,njuːklɪər 'fɪʃən/ *noun* the very great power made by splitting an atom: *A* **nuclear bomb** *is the most powerful weapon we have.*

O

obsessive /əbˈsesɪv/ *adjective* having a fixed idea from which the mind cannot be freed. **obsessively** *adverb*

occasionally /əˈkeɪʒnəli/ *adverb* happening from time to time

offence /əˈfens/ *noun* something that is wrong; a crime: *It is an* **offence** *to ride a bicycle at night without lights.*

operation /ɒpəˈreɪʃn/ *noun* 1 (*no plural*) the way a thing works; making something work: *The* **operation** *of a sewing-machine is easy.* 2 cutting a part of the body of someone who is ill: *an* **operation** *on her stomach*

out /aʊt/ *adverb* no longer fashionable: *Long skirts are* **out** *this year.*

outfit /ˈaʊtfɪt/ *noun* a set of clothes, especially for a special purpose: *The football team were wearing yellow* **outfits.**

outlaw /ˈaʊtlɔː/ *noun* (especially in former times) a criminal who lives in lonely areas and has not been caught by the police

P

pacemaker /ˈpeɪsmeɪkər/ *noun* a machine used to make weak or irregular heartbeats regular

painful /ˈpeɪnfəl/ *adjective* hurt a lot: *His head was very* **painful.**

parachute /ˈpærəʃuːt/ *noun* a large round piece of cloth that fills with air, and lets someone fall slowly to earth from an aeroplane

parallel /ˈpærəlel/ *adjective* always the same distance away from each other: **parallel** *lines*

paralyse /ˈpærəlaɪz/ *verb* (*present participle* **paralysing**, *past* **paralysed**) to prevent someone from being able to move some or all of his body: *The climber was* **paralysed** *in a fall, and couldn't walk.*

pass out /pɑːsˈaʊt/ *verb* to faint

patience /ˈpeɪʃns/ *noun* (*no plural*) the ability to wait calmly for a long time and not be made angry by delay: *Have* **patience**; *the bus will come soon.* **patiently** *adverb*: *He sat* **patiently** *waiting for the bus.*

patient /ˈpeɪʃnt/ *noun* a person who is ill: *The doctor visited his* **patients** *in hospital.*

patient /ˈpeɪʃnt/ *adjective* able to bear something or wait for something calmly: *I know your leg hurts, just be* **patient** *until the doctor arrives.*

peacock /ˈpiːkɒk/ *noun* a bird with a large brightly coloured tail

penicillin /ˌpenɪˈsɪlɪn/ *noun* a substance used as a medicine to destroy certain bacteria which cause illness in people and animals

performance /pəˈfɔːməns/ *noun* the acting of a part in a play or film in front of the public: *Her* **performance** *was very good. The* **performances** (= *times when the play is acted, film is shown, etc.*) *are on the 5th and 6th of this month.*

periscope /ˈperɪskəʊp/ *noun* a long tube with mirrors fitted in it so that people who are lower down, especially in submarines, can see what is above them

permit /pəˈmɪt/ *verb* (*present participle* **permitting**, *past* **permitted**) to allow: *Do you* **permit** *your children to smoke?* **permission** /pəˈmɪʃən/ *noun* (*no plural*): *You must* **ask permission** *if you want to go out.*

permit /ˈpɜːmɪt/ *noun* a piece of paper saying you are allowed to do something

persuade /pəˈsweɪd/ *verb* (*present participle* **persuading**, *past* **persuaded**) to talk with someone until they agree with what you say: *He* **persuaded** *her to go to school, even though she did not want to.*

persuasion /pəˈsweɪʒn/ *noun* (*no plural*): *After a lot of* **persuasion**, *she agreed to go.*

photograph /ˈfəʊtəgrɑːf/ *noun* a picture made with a camera

physician /fɪˈzɪʃn/ *noun* a doctor

picnic /ˈpɪknɪk/ *noun* an occasion when food is eaten somewhere outdoors

pie /paɪ/ *noun* a pastry case filled with meat or fruit, cooked in a deep dish

pink /pɪŋk/ *noun, adjective* the colour made by mixing red and white

pirate /ˈpaɪərət/ *noun* a robber of ships

pitch /pɪtʃ/ *noun* a part of a field on which games are played: *a football* **pitch**

pocket /ˈpɒkɪt/ *noun* a piece of material sewn onto clothes to make a little bag to keep things in

pond /pɒnd/ *noun* a pool of water: *a* **pond** *with fish in it*

popular /ˈpɒpjʊlər/ *adjective* liked by many people: *She is* **popular** *at school. This dance is* **popular** *with young people.*

popularity /ˌpɒpjʊˈlærəti/ *noun* (*no plural*) the quality of being well liked, approved of, or admired

port /pɔːt/ *noun* a harbour, or a town with a harbour

potato flakes /pəˈteɪtəʊ ˌfleɪks/ *noun* small, very thin pieces of potato

powder /ˈpaʊdər/ *noun* a substance in the form of very fine dry grains: *He stepped on the piece of chalk and crushed it to* **powder.**; *She used pink face* **powder.**

powder /ˈpaʊdər/ *verb* to put powder on

prescribe /prɪˈskraɪb/ *verb* to say what medicine or treatment a sick person should or must have: *The doctor prescribed a medicine for the child's stomach pains.* **prescription** /prɪˈskrɪpʃən/ *noun*

pretend /prɪˈtend/ *verb* to do something to make people believe something untrue: *He* **pretended** *that he was ill so that he could stay at home.*

print /prɪnt/ *verb* to press words and pictures on paper or cloth by machine: *You are reading a* **printed** *book.*

printer /ˈprɪntər/ *noun* a machine that prints computer information

print out /prɪnt ˈaʊt/ *verb* to make a printed record of computer information

producer /prəˈdjuːsər/ *noun* a person who has general control, especially of the money, for a film, but who does not direct the actors

professor /prəˈfesər/ *noun* a teacher of the highest class in a university

propose /prəˈpəʊz/ *verb* (*present participle* **proposing**, *past* **proposed**) to give as an idea: *He* **proposed** *that we should go for a walk.*

protection cream /prəˈtekʃn kriːm/ *noun* a substance put on the skin to guard it against the harmful effects of the sun

proud /praʊd/ *adjective* having a high opinion of yourself or of something that is yours: *He is* **proud** *of his daughter's ability to speak four languages. She is too* **proud** *to walk with the other children.*

provide /prəˈvaɪd/ *verb* (*present participle* **providing**, *past* **provided**) to give: *We* **provided** *food for the hungry children.* **provided (that)** if and only if: *You may go,* **provided (that)** *you come home by ten.*

public /ˈpʌblɪk/ *adjective* open to everyone; for the use of the people in general: *This is a* **public** *park, we can all go into it. I do not want to speak about it* **in public** (= *with other people there*).

public /ˈpʌblɪk/ *noun* (*no plural*) people: *The* **public** *can use this park.*

publicity /pʌˈblɪsəti/ *noun* public notice or attention: *The children's concert got a lot of* **publicity.**

publish /ˈpʌblɪʃ/ *verb* to print and sell: *This company* **publishes** *children's books.*

pull out /pʊl ˈaʊt/ *verb* to take out a tooth

pull over /pʊl ˈəʊvər/ *verb* of a vehicle, to move over to one side of the road

pulse /pʌls/ *noun* the beating of your heart: *The doctor felt her* **pulse** *on her wrist.*

punish /ˈpʌnɪʃ/ *verb* to make someone do something they do not like because they have done something wrong: *The teacher* **punished** *the noisy children by making them stay after school.*

put /pʊt/ *verb* (*present participle* **putting**, *past* **put**) to move to a place; to place: *He* **put** *the cups on the table.* **Put** *the lights* **on** (= turn them on); *it's too dark to read.*

put on /pʊt ˈɒn/ *verb* to cover the body with, especially clothes; get dressed in

R

radiation /ˌreɪdiˈeɪʃn/ *noun* the sending out of light and heat in all directions

radioactivity /ˌreɪdiəʊækˈtɪvɪti/ *noun* the quality, harmful to living things, that some simple substances have of giving out force by the breaking up of atoms. **radioactive** /ˌreɪdiəʊˈæktɪv/ *adjective*: *a highly* **radioactive** *material*

rarely /ˈreəli/ *adverb* not happening often

ray /reɪ/ *noun* a line of light: **rays** *of the sun*

react /riˈækt/ *verb* to act because of something that has happened: *How did your mother* **react** *to the news? She* **reacted** *by getting angry.* **reaction** /riˈækʃ:ən/ *noun*

receipt /rɪˈsiːt/ *noun* a piece of paper showing that you have paid for something: *Here is the* **receipt** *for your trainers.*

recently /ˈriːsntli/ *adverb* happening a short time ago: *I have been abroad* **recently.**

record /rɪˈkɔːd/ *verb* to store sounds electrically so that they can be listened to: *The songs were* **recorded** *by the radio company.* **recording** /rɪˈkɔːdɪŋ/ *noun*: *We made a* (tape) **recording** *of the songs.*

record /ˈrekɔːd/ *noun* 1 a round thin flat piece of plastic that stores sounds and which we play on a machine (**a record player**) to hear the sounds 2 something done better, quicker, etc. than anyone else has done it: *He holds the world* **record** *for the high jump. Can anyone* **break his record** (= do better)?

refund /rɪˈfʌnd/ *verb* to give money in repayment, in return for loss or damage

regret /rɪˈgret/ *verb* (*present participle* **regretting**, *past* **regretted**) to be sorry about something: *I* **regret** *spending so much money on a car. I* **regret** *to say I cannot come.*

rehearsal /rɪˈhɜːsəl/ *noun* the practice of a play, concert, etc.

relax /rɪˈlæks/ *verb* to become less worried, angry, tight, etc. *Don't worry about it, just try to* **relax**. **relaxˈation** *noun* (*no plural*)

replacement /rɪˈpleɪsmənt/ *noun* a thing or person put in the place of another: *We need a* **replacement** *for the teacher who left.*

reserve /rɪˈzɜːv/ *noun* a place where wild animals live and are protected: *Africa has many* **game reserves**.

revolver /rɪˈvɒlvəʳ/ *noun* a type of small gun

rhythm /ˈrɪðəm/ *noun* a regular sound like a drum in music: *I can't dance to music without a good* **rhythm**.

ribbon /ˈrɪbən/ *noun* a long narrow piece of material used for tying things: **ribbons** *in her hair*

ridiculous /rɪˈdɪkjʊləs/ *adjective* not reasonable; silly: *Don't be* **ridiculous** *– you can't play outside in the storm.*

ring /rɪŋ/ *noun* a round band especially of gold or silver, worn on the finger

ring /rɪŋ/ *verb* (*present participle* **ringing**, *past tense* **rang** /ræŋ/, *past participle* **rung** /rʌŋ/) to speak to on the telephone: *I* **rang** (**up**) *Peter to see if he could come to dinner.*

robbery /ˈrɒbəri/ *noun* the crime of taking someone else's money, goods, etc. from a person or place when it is not yours

role /rəʊl/ *noun* a character in a play or film: *He played the* **role** *of the old king in our school play.*

romance /rəʊˈmæns/ *noun* **1** being in love: *a* **romance** *between a king and a poor girl* **2** a story about love. **romantic** *adjective*

rough /rʌf/ *adjective* **1** not smooth; uneven: *a* **rough** *surface* **2** not calm or gentle; wild: *The sea was* **rough** *in the storm.* **3** not finished: *a* **rough** *drawing* ˈ**roughly** *adverb* **1** about: *I had* **roughly** *four kilometres to go.* **2** wildly: *He played* **roughly** *with the baby.*

row /rəʊ/ *noun* a line: *a* **row** *of pots on a shelf*

ruin /ˈruːɪn/ *verb* to destroy: *She poured water all over my painting, and* **ruined** *it.*

ruin /ˈruːɪn/ *noun* a building that has been destroyed: *We saw the* **ruins** *of the church.*

S

sack /sæk/ *noun* a large bag made of strong material: *a* **sack** *of rice*

sack /sæk/ *verb* to take away the job of; dismiss

sand /sænd/ *noun* (*no plural*) fine powder, usually white or yellow, made of rock, often found next to the sea and in deserts **sands** *plural noun* places covered with sand **sandy** *adjective* (**sandier, sandiest**): *a* **sandy** *shore*

sarong /səˈrɒŋ/ *noun* a loose skirt worn by women and men in Eastern countries

scene /siːn/ *noun* a short part of a play: *This play is divided into three acts, and each act has three* **scenes**.

script /skrɪpt/ *noun* the written form of a speech, play or broadcast

scriptwriter /ˈskrɪptˌraɪtəʳ/ *noun* a writer of scripts for films, broadcasts, etc.

secure /sɪˈkjʊəʳ/ *adjective* **1** safe: *I don't feel* **secure** *when I am alone at home.* **2** strong and fixed firmly: *This lock is* **secure**.

sensible /ˈsensəbəl/ *adjective* reasonable: *If you are* **sensible** *you will study for a year.*

sensitive /ˈsensɪtɪv/ *adjective:* quick to show or feel the effect of something

sentence /ˈsentəns/ *noun* a punishment for a criminal found guilty in court: *The* **sentence** *was ten years in prison.*

series /ˈsɪəriz/ *noun* (*plural* **series**) a number of things coming one after the other: *He saw a* **series** *of white arrows painted on the road.*

session /ˈseʃn/ *noun* a meeting of people for some purpose: *a dancing* **session**

shock /ʃɒk/ *noun* **1** the feeling caused by an unpleasant surprise; something causing this feeling: *It was a great* **shock** *for him when his wife died.* **2** a pain caused by electricity going through you: *An electric* **shock** *can kill you.*

shock /ʃɒk/ *verb* to cause unpleasant or angry surprise. **shocking** /ˈʃɒkɪŋ/ *adjective*

shoot /ʃuːt/ *verb* to make a film: *This film was* **shot** *in London.*

shoplifting /ˈʃɒpˌlɪftɪŋ/ *noun* taking goods from a shop without paying

show /ʃəʊ/ *noun* **1** a lot of things gathered together for people to see: *Many people went to see the flower* **show**. **2** something that people like to go and watch, especially a play, singing, etc.

shrink /ʃrɪŋk/ *verb* (*present participle* **shrinking**, *past tense* **shrank** /ʃræŋk/, *past participle* **shrunk** /ʃrʌŋk/) to get smaller: *The dress* **shrank** *when I washed it.*

sick /sɪk/ *adjective* bringing or wanting to bring food up from the stomach: *She feels* **sick** *in buses.* **be sick** to bring food up; vomit

sightseeing /ˈsaɪtsiːɪŋ/ *noun* going about as a tourist and visiting places of interest

silver /ˈsɪlvəʳ/ *noun* (*no plural*) **1** a soft shiny grey-white metal used for ornaments, old coins, etc. **2** the colour of this metal

simulate /ˈsɪmjəleɪt/ *verb* to give the effect or appearance of; imitate

sinister /ˈsɪnɪstəʳ/ threatening evil

size /saɪz/ *noun* how big something or someone is: *What* **size** *is your house? The two books were the same* **size**. *These shoes are* **size** *5.*

skin /skɪn/ *verb* to remove the skin from

slave /sleɪv/ *noun* a person who is owned by another person and has to work for him and has no freedom: *A long time ago, black people were taken to America as* **slaves**.

sleeve /sliːv/ *noun* part of a piece of clothing which covers the arm

slick back /slɪk ˈbæk/ *verb* to make, especially hair, flat and shiny with water, oil, etc.

slow down /sləʊ ˈdaʊn/ *verb* to make or become slower

smuggle /ˈsmʌgl/ *verb* (*present participle* **smuggling**, *past* **smuggled**) to bring things into a country secretly without paying the money that should be paid: *He was caught* **smuggling** *cameras into the country.* **smuggler** /ˈsmʌgləʳ/ *noun*

sore throat /sɔː ˈθrəʊt/ *noun* painful and aching inside the back of the mouth

sort out /sɔːt ˈaʊt/ *verb* to put things in order; solve

spade /speɪd/ *noun* an instrument used for digging

special effects /ˌspeʃəl ɪˈfekts/ *noun* things, such as recorded sounds, lights, man-made objects made to seem real, that are produced for films, broadcasts or the theatre

species /ˈspiːʃiz/ *noun* (*plural* **species**) sort; type: *a* **species** *of animal*

spectacular /spekˈtækjʊləʳ/ *adjective* grandly unusual, attracting excited notice

speculate /ˈspekjʊleɪt/ *verb* to think or talk about something without having the necessary facts; make guesses

spiky /ˈspaɪki/ *adjective* having long sharp points

sprain /spreɪn/ *verb* to damage a joint of your body by turning it suddenly: *He* **sprained** *his ankle when he fell.*

spread /spred/ *verb* to open out: *The bird* **spread** *its wings.*

stalactite /ˈstæləktaɪt/ *noun* a sharp downward pointing part of a cave roof like an icicle, formed over a long time by water containing minerals dropping from the roof

star /stɑːʳ/ *noun* **1** a small point of light that can be seen in the sky at night **2** a five-pointed shape (★) **3** a famous or very skilful actor/actress, sport person, singer, etc.: *a film* **star**/ *a football* **star**

star /stɑːʳ/ *verb* to have or appear as a main performer in a film, play, etc.

steal /stiːl/ *verb* (*present participle* **stealing**, *past tense* **stole** /stəʊl/, *past participle* **stolen**) **1** to take something that does not belong to you, without asking for it: *Who* **stole** *my money?*

stew /stjuː/ *noun* meat or fish and vegetables, cooked together in liquid

stick /stɪk/ *verb* (*present participle* **sticking**, *past* **stuck** /stʌk/) **1** to fix with a special substance (**glue**): *I* **stuck** *a stamp on the letter.*

stick up /stɪk ˈʌp/ *verb* (of hair) to come out straight upwards from the top of the head

stimulate /ˈstɪmjʊleɪt/ *verb* **1** to cause to become more active, grow faster, etc. **2** to encourage by exciting the mind or interest: *She was* **stimulated** *into new efforts.*

store /stɔːʳ/ *verb* (*present participle* **storing**, *past* **stored**) to put away or keep for use later: *I* **stored** *all the apples from our trees.*

store /stɔːʳ/ *noun* **1** things kept for future use: *a* **store** *of apples* **2** a large shop **3** a place for keeping things: *a* **store** *for furniture*

straight away /streɪt əˈweɪ/ *adverb* without waiting, now

straight off /streɪt ˈɒf/ *adverb infml* at once; without delay

stream /striːm/ *noun* **1** a small river **2** a flow: *a* **stream** *of cars*

stress /stres/ *noun* **1** (*no plural*) a state of difficulty: *The stress of working for examinations made him ill.* **2** (*plural* **stresses**) saying a word or a part of a word with special force: *In the word 'chemistry' the stress is on the first part of the word.*

strip /strip/ *noun* a long narrow piece of something: *a strip of paper*

stroll /strəʊl/ *verb* to walk slowly: *We strolled through the park.* **stroll** *noun*

struggle /'strʌgl/ *verb* (*present participle* **struggling**, *past* **struggled**) to fight: *I struggled to get free.*

style /staɪl/ *noun* **1** a way of doing something: *a hair style* **2** the way of dressing that everyone likes at a special time: *That dress is in the latest style.* **3** a sort or type: *a new style of car*

substance /'sʌbstəns/ *noun* a sort of material: *Salt is a substance we use in cooking.*

successful /sək'sesfəl/ *adjective* having done something one has tried to do: *Making my cake was very successful.*

suck /sʌk/ *verb* to draw liquid into the mouth: *The baby was sucking milk from its mother.*

suit /suːt/ *verb* to be right for; look nice when worn: *It suits me if you come to work at eight o'clock. That dress suits you.*

sun /sʌn/ *noun* the large ball of fire in the sky which gives light and heat: *The sun rose at six o'clock. Sit in the sun and get warm.*

sunny /'sʌni/ *adjective* (**sunnier, sunniest**): *The day was bright and sunny.*

sunglasses /'sʌn,glɑːsɪz/ *noun* glasses with dark glass in them to protect the eyes from the sun

suntan /'sʌntæn/ *noun* the brownness of the skin after the effects of sunshine

supermarket /'suːpəmɑːkɪt/ *noun* a big shop where you choose what you want and pay as you go out

supervise /'suːpəvaɪz/ *verb* (*present participle* **supervising**, *past* **supervised**) to watch over people while they work, to see that they are doing the right thing: *The teacher supervised our drawing class.*

surfing /'sɜːfɪŋ/ *noun* the sport of riding over waves near the shore on a special narrow board (surfboard)

suspect /sə'spekt/ *verb* to think that something is true, though you do not know: *He seems poor, but I suspect that he has quite a lot of money.*

suspect /'sʌspekt/ *noun* someone who is thought to have done wrong: *The police have taken the suspect to the police station.*

suspend /sə'spend/ *verb* to delay: *We suspended the building work during the rain.*

suspense /sə'spens/ *noun* (*no plural*) delay which frightens or excites people: *Tell us what happened, we're all waiting in suspense.*

suspicious /sə'spɪʃəs/ *adjective* feeling that something is wrong: *I am suspicious of that woman – I think she may have stolen something from our shop.*

sweat /swet/ *noun* (*no plural*) water which comes out of your skin: *Sweat poured down his face as he ran.*

swell /swel/ *verb* (*present participle* **swelling**, *past tense* **swelled**, *past participle* **swollen** /'swəʊlən/) to become larger: *A bee has stung my hand and it is swelling up. After the rain, the river swelled.* **swelling** *noun*: *The bee sting has left a swelling on my hand.*

swinging /'swɪŋɪŋ/ *adjective* active, fashionably modern and full of life

symptom /'sɪmptəm/ *noun* a sign of something, especially an illness: *Fever is a symptom of many illnesses.*

T

tan /tæn/ *verb* to make or become brown, especially by sunlight. **tan** *noun* suntan

tattoo /tæ'tuː/ *verb* to make a pattern on the skin by pricking it and putting colouring substances on it. **tattoo** *noun*

tear /teər/ *verb* (*past tense* **tore** /tɔːr/, *past participle* **torn** /tɔːn/) to pull into pieces; make a hole in

technician /tek'nɪʃn/ *noun* a person who works with machines or instruments: *Anne is training to be a technician.*

technology /tek'nɒlədʒi/ *noun* (*no plural*) using the knowledge we get through science to make things in factories, build things, etc: *the new technology of micro* (= very small) *computers*

teddy boy /'tedi bɔɪ/ *noun* in Britain, especially in the 1950s, a young man who dressed in a style similar to that of the early 20th century, wearing a long loose jacket, narrow trousers and thick soft shoes

telephone /'telɪfəʊn/ *or* **phone** /fəʊn/ *noun* **1** (*no plural*) a way of carrying the sound of a person's voice by electricity over a wire or by radio: *We told him the news by telephone.* **2** the instrument used to carry the sounds: *Please answer the telephone* (= pick it up when it rings and speak into it).

temperature /'temprətʃər/ *noun* the amount of heat or cold: *In hot weather the temperature gets very high. When I was ill, I had a high temperature; I felt very hot.*

theory /'θɪəri/ *noun* (*plural* **theories**) an idea that tries to explain something: *One theory about the moon is that it is a piece broken off the earth.*

think /θɪŋk/ *verb* (*past* **thought** /θɔːt/) **1** to use the mind: *Have you thought about what job you are going to do?* **2** to have an opinion; believe something: *What do you think of my singing? I think it will be hot today. I couldn't think of* (= remember) *his name.* **think (something) out** to consider carefully and in detail (a plan, problem, etc.)

thread /θred/ *verb* to put a thread through a needle

tie /taɪ/ *verb* (*present participle* **tying**, *past* **tied**) to fasten something with string or rope: *Can you tie up this parcel for me?*

tonsils /'tɒnsəlz/ *noun* two small organs at the side of the throat near the back of the tongue

tool /tuːl/ *noun* an instrument which helps us to do work

toothache /'tuːθeɪk/ *noun* (*no plural*) a pain in a tooth: *I've had toothache all day.*

tortoise /'tɔːtəs/ *noun* an animal with a body covered by a round hard shell

tough /tʌf/ *adjective* **1** hard; not easy to bite or tear: *This meat is tough. Leather is a tough material.* **2** strong and brave

tradition /trə'dɪʃn/ *noun* old customs or knowledge passed on from parents to their children: *It is a tradition that the young people look after the old in their family.* **traditional** /trə'dɪʃnl/ *adjective* **traditionally** *adverb*

trailer /'treɪlər/ *noun* a two-wheeled cart pulled by a car, etc.

trainers /'treɪnəz/ *noun* strong sports shoes with a heavy rubber bottom

transfer /træns'fɜːr/ *verb* to move people or things from one place to another: *His employer transferred him to another office.*

treasure /'treʒər/ *noun* (*no plural*) a collection of gold, silver, etc.: *The treasure dug out of the earth was a box of gold coins.*

treat /triːt/ *verb* **1** to behave towards: *He treated the animal cruelly.* **2** to give medicine as a doctor: *to treat an illness*

treatment /'triːtmənt/ *noun* the act, manner or method of treating someone: *He's gone to hospital for special treatment.*

trendy /'trendi/ *adjective* very fashionable

trick /trɪk/ *noun* **1** an action meant to deceive **2** a clever act done to amuse people: *I can do magic tricks.*

trip /trɪp/ *noun* a short journey from one place to another

try /traɪ/ *verb* (*present participle* **trying**, *past* **tried**) **1** to do one's best to do something: *He tried to climb the tree, but he could not.* **2** to test something: *Have you tried this chocolate? She tried on the dress to see if it would fit.*

tumble /'tʌmbəl/ *verb* to fall or roll over suddenly, helplessly or in disorder; *to tumble down the stairs; The children tumbled off the bus.*

turn /tɜːn/ *verb* **1** to go or make something go round and round: *The wheels were turning. Will you turn the wheel to the right?* **2** to change or make something change position or direction

turn off /tɜːn 'ɒf/ *verb* to stop a flow of (water, gas, electricity, etc.): **Turn off** *the television!*

turn on /tɜːn 'ɒn/ *verb* to cause (water, gas, electricity, etc.) to flow: *He turned on the light.*

turn to /tɜːn 'tuː/ *verb* **1** to go to for help **2** to look at the stated page in a book

turtle /'tɜːtl/ *noun* an animal which has a hard round shell over its body, and lives mainly in the sea

twin /twɪn/ *noun* one of two children born of the same mother at the same time

U

uncomfortable /ʌn'kʌmftəbəl/ *adjective* not comfortable

unconvincing /ˌʌnkən'vɪnsɪŋ/ *adjective* not easy to believe or accept: *an unconvincing excuse*

unfashionable /ˌʌnˈfæʃnəbl/ *adjective* a way of dressing that does not follow the style or fashion popular at that particular time

unfriendly /ˌʌnˈfrendlɪ/ *adjective* not friendly: *Why is she so* **unfriendly**?

unhappy /ˌʌnˈhæpɪ/ *adjective* (**unhappier, unhappiest**) not happy; sad: *She looked* **unhappy** *after she read the letter.*

unpleasant /ˌʌnˈpleznt/ *adjective* not nice or pleasant: *That drink has an* **unpleasant** *taste, I don't like it.*

unsuccessful /ˌʌnsʌkˈsesfəl/ *adjective* having not been able to do something one has tried to do

untidy /ˌʌnˈtaɪdɪ/ *adjective* (**untidier, untidiest**) not tidy: *Her room was* **untidy** – *there were clothes all over the floor.*

V

valley /ˈvælɪ/ *noun* low ground between two hills or mountains

valuable /ˈvæljuəbəl/ *adjective* worth a lot: *This house is very* **valuable**; *it would cost you a lot of money.*

VDU /ˌviːdiːˈjuː/ *noun* visual display unit; an apparatus with a screen which shows information from a computer

velvet /ˈvelvɪt/ *noun* (*no plural*) a type of cloth with a soft surface

version /ˈvɜːʃn/ *noun* a story told by one person compared with the same story told by another: *I have heard two* **versions** *of the accident.*

vocal /ˈvəʊkəl/ *adjective* **1** connected with or produced by or for the voice **2** produced by the voice, sung or spoken aloud

W

waist /weɪst/ *noun* the narrow part of the body between the chest and the legs: *Ann wore a belt around her* **waist**.

walk /wɔːk/ *verb* to move on the feet at the usual speed: *We* **walk** *to school each day.*

walk out /wɔːk ˈaʊt/ *verb* to leave suddenly, especially as an expression of disapproval

weak /wiːk/ *adjective* **1** not strong in body or character: *She was* **weak** *after her illness.* **2** containing a lot of water

weird /wɪəd/ *adjective* strange; unusual: **weird** *clothes*

well-directed /ˌwel dəˈrektɪd/ *adjective* of a film which has been directed in the best and most interesting way

wheelchair /ˈwiːltʃeəʳ/ *noun* a chair with large wheels used by a person who cannot walk

widow /ˈwɪdəʊ/ *noun* a woman whose husband is dead

wig /wɪg/ *noun* a covering for the head, made of hair from other people or animals

wildlife /ˈwaɪldlaɪf/ *noun* animals and plants which are living in their natural surroundings: *We started a campaign to protect the* **wildlife** *in the area.*

wind /wɪnd/ *noun* air moving quickly: *The* **wind** *blew the leaves off the trees.* **windy** *adjective*

windsurfing /ˈwɪndsɜːfɪŋ/ *noun* (*no plural*) the sport of riding along on the sea on a narrow board with a sail

wipe /waɪp/ *verb* (*present participle* **wiping**, *past* **wiped**) to make dry or clean with a cloth: *Will you* **wipe** *the table? She* **wiped** *the marks* **off** *the table.*

wise /waɪz/ *adjective* (**wiser, wisest**) having or showing good sense and cleverness: **wise** *advice.* **wisdom** /ˈwɪzdəm/ *noun She showed great* **wisdom**. **wisely** *adverb: to act* **wisely**

workshop /ˈwɜːkʃɒp/ *noun* a room or place as in a factory where things are produced, repairs are done, etc.

wrinkle /ˈrɪŋkl/ *noun* a line or fold on a surface: *Grandfather has many* **wrinkles** *on his face.* **wrinkled** *adjective*

wrist /rɪst/ *noun* the joint between the hand and the lower part of the arm

X

x-ray /ˈeks reɪ/ *noun* a photograph of the inside of your body, taken with a special unseen light: *The* **x-ray** *showed that the boy's leg was broken.*

x-ray /ˈeks reɪ/ *verb* to photograph by x-ray

Z

zany /ˈzeɪnɪ/ *adjective* foolish in a very funny or strange way: *He made us laugh with his* **zany** *tricks.*